WINCHESTER
CURIOSITIES

WINCHESTER
CURIOSITIES

DAVID HILLIAM

First published in 2008 by
The History Press
The Mill, Brimscombe Port,
Stroud, Gloucestershire, GL5 2QG
www.thehistorypress.co.uk

Reprinted 2010

Title page photograph: The Arms of the
City of Winchester.

British Library Cataloguing in Publication Data
A catalogue record for this book is available from the
British Library.

ISBN 978-07509-4890-6

Typeset in 10.5/13.5 Photina.
Typesetting and origination by
The History Press.
Printed and bound in Great Britain by
Marston Book Services Limited, Oxford

CONTENTS

ACKNOWLEDGEMENTS & THANKS

In preparing this book I owe thanks to many people. In particular I am grateful to the following: The Revd James Bates, the former Master of St Cross Hospital, for permission to use photographs of St Cross Hospital, the Church of St Cross and the 'Wayfarer's Dole'; Rodney Browne (Books and Maps), for providing rare source material; Dr John Crook (info@john-crook.com), for his ready help in allowing me to use his photographs on pages viii, 16, 30, 32, 33, 35, 37, 64 and 66; Simon Fletcher, without whose support and encouragement this book would not have been published; my wife Mary Hilliam, not only for the photograph of the Rufus Stone but also for invaluable help with proofing and indexing; Paul Morgan, of Messrs Warren & Son of Winchester, for giving me permission to use photographs from the former well-known *Warren's Guide to Winchester* on pages 6, 9, 10, 23, 40, 41, 46, 50, 51, 73 and 92; the family of C.G. Stevens, for permission to use the illustrations on pages 60–61, 63 and 96–97 (C.G. Stevens was a 17-year-old Winchester scholar in 1920 when he drew these items for a Winchester College publication); and to Claire Tomalin for advice on the Giles King Lyford plaque. The drawing of John Keats on page 101 comes from London Stories by 'John O'London'. All photographs and drawings not mentioned above are my own.

David Hilliam

INTRODUCTION

A definitive book on Winchester would be impossible – so this collection of 'curiosities' is inevitably and unashamedly selective, perhaps quirkily so. It picks out items of special interest for a first-time visitor. But hopefully, too, it calls attention to things that can be missed even by those who are already familiar with this ancient city and its superb cathedral.

Part One is a selection of some of the main things to see in the cathedral, which contains – among many other items – the oldest royal bones in England and memories of one of the most popular of all the Saxon saints – St Swithun.

Part Two is a selection of things to see in the city. Like many old towns, Winchester is a place to poke into and examine at leisure – often yielding surprising curiosities.

At the end of this book is a timeline covering almost 2,500 years – about 600 generations. During that long tract of time, Winchester has been the stage on which scores of kings, queens, saints and sinners have played their dramatic part in our history. For centuries, Winchester was the most important place in England.

This book is intended as an appetite-whetter. Winchester has such a rich historic past that you could literally spend a lifetime trying to unearth its secrets. It's hoped that these pages will prove an unusual and worthwhile starting point.

David Hilliam

Wooden roof of the tower. (*John Crook*)

AN ODD PUZZLE IN LATIN

In the very centre of the cathedral tower roof (in the middle of the crossing of the nave and transepts) is a circular trapdoor called the corona, and around this is a curiously ingenious Latin sentence:

sint DoMVs hVIVs pII reges nVtrItII regInae nVtrICes pIae

Translated, this means: 'May pious kings be the nursing fathers of this house and pious queens its nursing mothers.' Nowadays, of course, we would put 'U' instead of 'V', but in earlier centuries a 'V' was quite usual. But importantly, in this sentence, taken from Isaiah ch. 49 v. 23, the 'v's have a double purpose.

If we rearrange the letters in order of magnitude, this gives us MDCVVVVV III III III – which produces the Roman numerals for the year of its construction – 1634. In fact, this elaborate roof was not made until the reign of Charles I (1625–49).

You need to stand in the centre of the quire stalls to see this, and binoculars may be useful to help you enjoy this quirky Latin puzzle. In each corner is a shield with the arms of the cathedral (see opposite page). Are these correct versions?

PART ONE

WINCHESTER CATHEDRAL & CLOSE

THE ARMS OF THE SEE OF WINCHESTER

Correct version   Incorrect version

Winchester Cathedral is dedicated to the Holy Trinity; St Peter and St Paul, and St Swithun. The arms of the See of Winchester, as shown above, contain the symbolic keys of St Peter (who was given the 'Keys of the Kingdom of Heaven'), and the symbolic sword of St Paul (who was beheaded with a sword).

In heraldic terms, these arms are: *gules* (red) *two keys addorsed bendwise the upper argent* (silver) *and the other or* (gold) *and between them, a sword bendwise sinister, blade silver, pommel and hilt gold.*

The arms shown above can be found on bosses in all four corners of the vaulted roof of the tower, at the central crossing of the nave and transepts (*see* opposite page). However, heraldically, the arms displayed there are all incorrect! Properly, the sword and keys should be shown the other way round – with the handles of the keys in the bottom right, and the sword with its hilt in the bottom left (*bendwise sinister*).

Of the two versions shown above, the left one is the correct one: the one on the right is wrong. You will find both versions as you look round the cathedral.

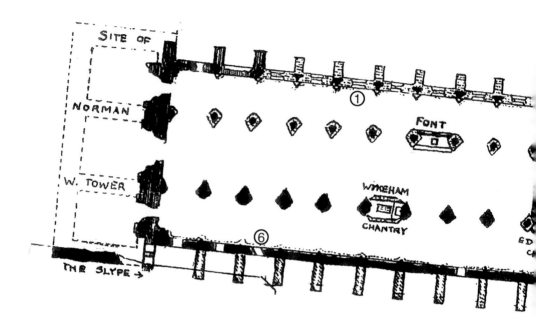

This plan of Winchester Cathedral is particularly interesting as it shows the site of the Norman towers which were pulled down in the fourteenth century when the present west front was put in place. There are so many things to find in the cathedral, but this plan is simplified simply to show the chantries and six memorials mentioned in this book:

1. The gravestone and window in memory of Jane Austen

2. The 'Rufus Tomb' – now thought to be that of Henry of Blois

3. Statue of Joan of Arc

4. Bust of William Walker, the diver

5. The Silkstede Chapel, where Izaak Walton is buried and where the stained-glass window in his memory can be found

6. Memorial to Joseph Warton, shown teaching boys of Winchester College

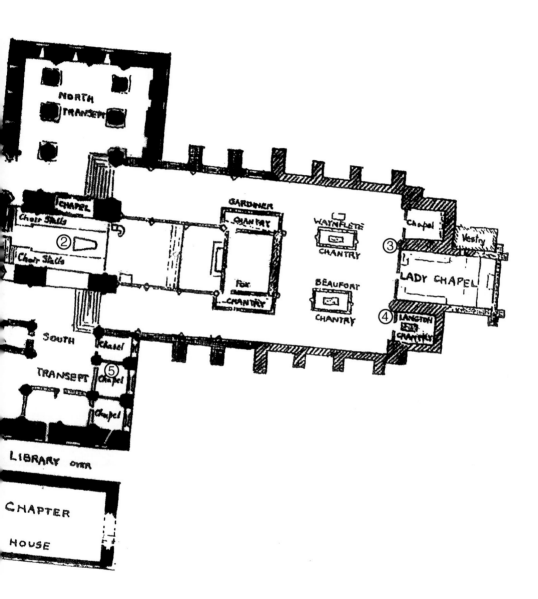

WHOSE STATUE IS AT THE TOP OF THE CATHEDRAL?

The cathedral's West Front was constructed in the 1360s by Bishop Edington. Its balcony was designed for bishops at church festivals as they came out to bless the assembled crowds below. Sadly, the niches on this façade were stripped of their statues at the time of the Reformation, but there is a statue to be seen at the very top of the central gable. But which saint is it?

Surprisingly, it is not a saint at all but a Victorian statue of William of Wykeham, the man who transformed the nave and founded Winchester College and New College, Oxford. Binoculars are useful to see him clearly, as well as the imps, devils and gargoyles which are just visible in high places on this West Front. (*See* p. 7 for drawing of Wykeham's statue.)

The West Front of the cathedral, with some of the grotesques which adorn it.

THE LONGEST GOTHIC CATHEDRAL IN THE WORLD

At 556ft (169.5m), Winchester Cathedral is the longest Gothic cathedral in the world. There are longer Classical cathedrals, and longer modern cathedrals, but Winchester holds the record among cathedrals built before the Renaissance.

The last extension to the length of Winchester Cathedral came early in the sixteenth century, when Elizabeth of York, Queen of Henry VII, paid for the Lady Chapel at the east end to be lengthened after she had given birth to her first son, Prince Arthur, in Winchester and the infant had been baptised at the cathedral's font.

FIVE CATHEDRALS WHICH ARE SHORTER THAN WINCHESTER . . .

St Albans Cathedral	550ft
Canterbury Cathedral	547ft
Ely Cathedral	537ft
Westminster Abbey	529ft
York Minster	524ft

. . . AND THREE WHICH ARE LONGER

St Peter's, Rome	719ft
Liverpool Anglican Cathedral	636ft
St John the Divine, New York	601ft

. . . BUT WINCHESTER MIGHT HAVE BEEN EVEN LONGER!

The original Norman cathedral, built by Bishop Walkelyn, stretched another 40ft further westward. A stone set in the wall to the south of the present West Front (see below) marks where the earlier west end finished. It is thought that there were two huge towers – probably resembling the tower at Ely Cathedral. Bishop Edington demolished these towers in about 1360, when he restructured the nave and replaced them with the present west end. The site of the original west end is shown on the plan on pp. 2–3.

Plaque showing the original length of the cathedral.

A MASSIVE MEDIEVAL MAKEOVER

Few buildings anywhere in the world have undergone such a gigantic transformation as Winchester Cathedral in the fourteenth century.

The two plans below show the design of the original Norman bays (the sections between each pair of pillars in the nave) compared with the Perpendicular design which we see today. The Norman work was done between 1079 and 1093. Most of the makeover was done between 1360 and 1404, when William of Wykeham died, but work continued for about another fifty years.

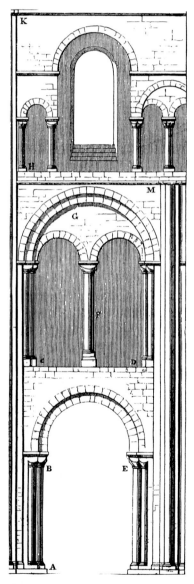

The old Norman plan.

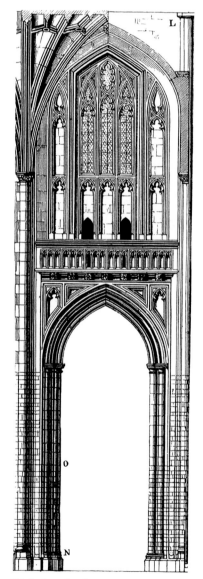

Wykeham's plan.

THE OLD CATHEDRAL TRANSFORMED INTO A NEW ONE

As shown on the opposite page, the nave of Winchester Cathedral was completely transformed in the fourteenth century. Bishop Edington (bishop from 1346 to 1366) began the work in about 1360, and William of Wykeham (bishop from 1366 to 1404) continued the work.

It was a huge undertaking, and Wykeham was over seventy years of age when he began the task of pulling down and then rebuilding the nave. The cathedral became virtually a brand new building under Wykeham's expert direction. Before he had entered the church, he had made his name as Chief Warden and Surveyor of Royal Castles for King Edward III.

The King made Wykeham his Private Secretary, then Keeper of the Privy Seal, and in 1367 he became Chancellor. Wykeham became the richest and most powerful man in the country. It was his personal generosity that enabled Winchester's 'new' cathedral to be funded.

The beautiful fan vaulting, enriched with so many bosses (*see* pp. 26–9) was also begun at this time.

The impetus for change ceased after the middle of the fifteenth century, so that the transepts were left untouched. As a result, visitors today can appreciate the bold, simple Norman work in the north and south transepts as well as appreciate the elaborate Perpendicular work in the main body of the cathedral.

Statue of William of Wykeham at the pinnacle of the gable on the West Front.

HOOKS USED FOR A ROYAL WEDDING

It is impossible to put into words the sheer beauty of Winchester's long nave, with its intricate fan vaulting, its innumerable bosses and seemingly endless bays of exquisite Perpendicular carving. However, do not miss the practical large iron hooks, which are set into the pillars about halfway up. They were fixed into the masonry specially for holding a series of magnificent tapestries, which adorned the cathedral for the marriage of Queen Mary Tudor to Philip of Spain on 25 July 1554 (St James's Day).

Today, sixteen modern batik banner paintings illustrating the Creation have been designed and made by Thetis Blacker (1927–2006), and these striking images, calling to mind the Biblical themes of the Old and New Testament, can be seen on special occasions. But the hooks on which they hang are a reminder of the time when Philip of Spain became – for a few years – King of England. He enjoyed the title, though he had no power in England and remained in this country for only a few months.

The nave of Winchester Cathedral.

ROYAL OCCASIONS IN THE CATHEDRAL

The marriage of Queen Mary Tudor and Philip of Spain was only one of many great royal occasions that have taken place in the cathedral. Among some of the other main events that have taken place here during the last 900 years are:

1093   The dedication of Walkelin's new Norman cathedral on Easter Sunday – 8 April. For about 200 years, the kings of England made a practice of 'crown-wearing' at Easter in Winchester, a custom started by William the Conqueror.

1194   Richard I was crowned for a second time here, on Easter Sunday, after having been ransomed and released from captivity in Austria on his way back from the Third Crusade to the Holy Land. His mother, Eleanor of Aquitaine, was present at the ceremony.

1207   The future King Henry III, son of King John, was baptised here at the black marble font (see pp. 10–11). In later years, Henry liked to call himself 'Henry of Winchester'.

1403   King Henry IV married his second wife, Joan of Navarre, at the cathedral.

1486   Prince Arthur, son of King Henry VII and heir to the throne, was baptised at the cathedral.

1554   Probably the greatest royal occasion of all – the marriage of Queen Mary to Philip of Spain.

1979   Queen Elizabeth II distributed the Royal Maundy in Winchester Cathedral to commemorate the 900th anniversary of its foundation.

This chair was used by Mary Tudor at her wedding to Philip of Spain. It can still be seen in the cathedral.

THREE BUTCHERED BOYS, A GOLDEN CUP AND THREE LUCKY GIRLS

A gift to the cathedral by Bishop Henry of Blois (nephew of William the Conqueror and Bishop of Winchester 1129–73) is the magnificent square twelfth-century font standing on the north side of the nave. It is made from black marble and comes from Tournai in Belgium.

The rich Norman carvings have been given several interpretations, but it is agreed that they show three legends of St Nicholas – the original 'Santa Claus'. The carvings are intricate and a little confusing at first sight, but it is well worthwhile spending time to work out the details.

1. The miracle of the three butchered boys

In the middle of the west side are two scenes showing one of St Nicholas's most dramatic miracles in which he brought three boys back to life after they had been chopped up by a butcher intending to turn them into meat pies.

The font shows the butcher wielding an axe, with his wife standing behind him, just about to cut off the boys' heads: the boys are shown vertically, lying in bed. Then, to the right of this, St Nicholas – identified by mitre and crozier – is busily restoring the boys back to life.

The Norman font, showing butchered boys and drowned child on the left side, and the legend of the three girls on the right.

2. The miracle of the drowned child and the golden cup

On each side of the butchered boys' miracle are two scenes showing the story of how St Nicholas brought a drowned child back to life. The story has several versions. This carving tells how a childless nobleman promised to give a golden cup to Nicholas if he were granted his wish to have a son and heir. The son was born and the nobleman set off by boat to take the golden cup to Myra, where Nicholas was bishop. Unfortunately, the child fell overboard and was drowned with the cup in his hand. Miraculously, St Nicholas rescued both the child and the cup.

On the right of this west side of the font, the nobleman is depicted with sailors in a boat, and the child is seen lying at the bottom of the sea. On the extreme left, St Nicholas is shown restoring the boy to life.

Detail from the miracle of the drowned child, showing St Nicholas and sailors in a ship with a splendid prow.

3. The legend of the three girls

The south side of the font contains a scene showing St Nicholas's famous generosity. The story tells how a father was so desperately poor that he was about to sell his three daughters to a brothel. When St Nicholas heard about this, he secretly threw three bags of gold into the poor man's window, thus providing dowries for them.

The font shows Nicholas giving a bag of gold to the father, who is on his knees. Behind the father are his three daughters, and behind them is a man holding a hawk in his hand – probably hoping to marry one of the newly-rich girls.

This story began the legend that 'Santa Claus' is responsible for the appearance of Christmas presents. Also the pawnbrokers' traditional sign of the three balls is a symbolic representation of St Nicholas's gift of three bags of gold.

SAINT AUGUSTINE, KING DAVID AND JANE AUSTEN

Jane Austen, with her lively sense of humour and sharp appreciation of the absurd, would surely have given a wry smile if she had known that a stained-glass window, depicting St Augustine, would be placed in her memory at the cathedral on the flimsy connection that her surname can be seen as a shortened version of 'Augustine'. As for King David – he can (just) be seen as an emblem of creative writing. And then, perhaps somewhat tortuously, the other figures depicted in the window are the sons of Korah (*see* 2 Chronicles, 20.19) who carry scrolls with quotations from psalms, reminding us of Jane's religious virtues.

This memorial window can be seen in the north aisle, almost opposite the font described on pp. 10 and 11, and set into the floor just below this window is the extraordinary black marble gravestone put there by Jane Austen's family, and written by her brother Henry. Astonishingly, it makes no mention whatsoever of the fact that Jane ever wrote or published anything. It reads:

In Memory of
JANE AUSTEN,
youngest daughter of the late
Revd GEORGE AUSTEN,
formerly Rector of Steventon in this County
she departed this Life on the 18th July 1817,
aged 41, after a long illness supported with
the patience and the hopes of a Christian.

The benevolence of her heart,
the sweetness of her temper, and
the extraordinary endowments of her mind
obtained the regard of all who knew her, and
the warmest love of her intimate connections.

Their grief is in proportion to their affection
they know their loss to be irreparable,
but in their deepest affliction they are consoled
by a firm though humble hope that her charity,
devotion, faith and purity have rendered
her soul acceptable in the sight of her
REDEEMER.

In 1872, to make up for this strange lack of reference to Jane's writings, her nephew, the Revd James-Edward Austen-Leigh, had a brass memorial tablet placed on the wall against the marble slab on the floor. Even then, the reference to her fame as a writer is minimal, to say the least:

JANE AUSTEN
Known to many by her
writings, endeared to
her family by the
varied charms of her
Character and ennobled
by Christian faith
and piety, was born
at Steventon in the
County of Hants Dec.
xvi mdcclxxv, and buried
in this Cathedral
July xxiv mdcccxvii
'She openeth her
mouth with wisdom
and in her tongue is
the law of kindness.'
Prov. xxxi v.xxvi

The window itself, designed by the well-known stained-glass artist C.E. Kempe, was erected in 1900 by public subscription.

But all three memorials are curiously and disappointingly cool about Jane Austen's wonderful novels, which include *Pride and Prejudice*, *Sense and Sensibility* and *Emma*, among many others which have delighted generations of readers for almost two centuries.

It is said that some years after Austen's death, a verger of Winchester Cathedral was puzzled why so many people asked him to show them the grave of Jane Austen. He asked: 'Was there anything particular about that lady?' Indeed there was.

TWENTY-EIGHT SAINTS, THIRTEEN BISHOPS, SIX KINGS, QUEEN EMMA, EMPRESS MATILDA AND QUEEN VICTORIA

The intricately carved Great Screen behind the altar is one of the finest in the country. Its niches contain not only angels and biblical saints but also statues of famous people who have had direct links with Winchester. Cromwell's soldiers destroyed the original medieval carvings in the seventeenth century, so what we see today are nineteenth-century replacements.

Some of the people chosen to be placed in these niches were controversial at the time they were added to the screen – and there are some surprises. It is worth taking time to study this remarkable collection of statues.

In the centre is a carving of Jesus Christ on the cross, with the Virgin Mary on his right, and St John on his left. Above the arms of the cross are four archangels (from left to right: Uriel, Gabriel, Michael and Raphael). Then there are six angels, twenty-eight saints, thirteen bishops, six kings, three queens and, somewhat unexpectedly, Izaak Walton, John Keble and Earl Godwin.

On the page opposite is a complete list, with dates – and the following two pages contain a photograph of the complete Great Screen and a plan showing where each figure is to be found.

Statue of King Canute (Cnut) on the Great Screen.

WHO'S WHO ON THE GREAT SCREEN

FOUR ARCHANGELS
Gabriel
Michael
Raphael
Uriel

TWENTY-EIGHT SAINTS
Alphege, d. 951
Ambrose, *c.* 339–97
Agnes *c.* 292 – *c.* 304
Anne, mother of the Virgin Mary
Augustine, 354–430
Benedict, *c.* 480–*c.* 547
Birinus, d. *c.* 650
Boniface, *c.* 675–754
Catherine, d. 307
Cecilia, third century
Eadburga, d. 960
Ealswith, d. 902
Edmund, King & Martyr 841–70
Ethelwold, bishop 963–84
Faith, third century (?)
Edward the Confessor, reigned 1043–66
Giles, d. 710
Gregory the Great, *c.* 540–604
Grimbald, *c.* 825–901
Hedda, bishop 676–705
Jerome, *c.* 342–420
John, Apostle, late first century
Laurence, d. 619
Margaret, (no date)
Paul, d. *c.* 65
Peter, d. *c.* 64
Stephen, d. *c.* 35
Swithun, *c.* 805–62

THIRTEEN BISHOPS OF WINCHESTER
(*Dates indicate term of office*)
Lancelot Andrewes, 1619–26
Cardinal Beaufort, 1404–47
Henry of Blois, 1128–71
Daniel, 705–44
Edington, 1345–66
Fox, 1501–28
Ken, Bishop of Bath & Wells 1685–91
Godfrey de Lucy, 1189–1204
Stigand, 1047–70
Walkelin, 1070–98
Wayneflete, 1447–86
Cardinal Wolsey, 1529–30
Wykeham, 1367–1404

SIX KINGS
(*Dates indicate length of reign*)
Alfred the Great, 871–99
Cnut (Canute), 1016–35
Edgar, 959–75
Edward I, 1272–1307
Egbert, 802–39
Cynegils, 611–43

THREE QUEENS
Emma (wife of Ethelred & Canute) d. 1052
Matilda, 'Lady of the English', reigned
  1141
Victoria, reigned 1837–1901

THREE OTHERS
Izaac Walton (1593–1683)
John Keble (1792–1866)
Earl Godwin, d. 1053

THE GREAT SCREEN

The intricate stonework of the Great Screen, or reredos, contains some of the most magnificent carving in the world. The stone statues, nineteenth-century replacements of the medieval originals, inevitably attract our attention, but the beautiful patterns of the canopies are often overlooked. These are late Gothic, carved in the middle of the sixteenth century.

The Great Screen. (*John Crook*)

Saint Ambrose · Bishop Ken · Izaak Walton · Saint Gregory the Great · John Keble · Bishop Andrewes · Saint Peter · Uriel · Gabriel · Spire · Michael · Raphael · Saint Paul · Bishop Daniel · Saint Alphege · Saint Jerome · Saint Grimbald · Saint Boniface · Saint Augustine

Angel · Angel

Henry of Blois · Saint Stephen · Cardinal Beaufort · King Egbert · Saint Benedict · William of Wykeham · Saint Ealswith · Saint Swithun · Angel · Angel · The Virgin Mary · our Lord Jesus Christ · Bishop Fox's Emblem of the Pelican · Saint John · Angel · Angel · Saint Birinus · Bishop Wayneflete · Saint Eadburga · Saint Giles · Bishop Fox · Bishop Edington · Saint Laurence · Cardinal Wolsey

King Edgar · Queen Matilda · King Edward the Confessor · Cnut · Bp. Godfrey Lucy · DOOR · Bishop Walkelin · Queen Emma · Saint Hedda · St. Margaret · St. Catherine · St. Anne · The Holy Family · St. Agnes · St. Cecilia · St. Faith · Altar · Saint Ethelwold · Queen Victoria · Archbishop Stigand · DOOR · Alfred the Great · Earl Godwin · Saint Edmund the King · King Cynegils · King Edward The Elder

Plan of the statues on the Great Screen.

A SILENT REMINDER OF A TERRIBLE DEED

It comes as a surprise to see a twentieth-century statue of Joan of Arc in the north-east corner of the cathedral. Why should she be remembered here?

Joan's link with Winchester is through Cardinal Beaufort, Bishop of Winchester, who led the trial proceedings against her. In 1431, she was burned as a witch in Rouen marketplace – and the rich and powerful 'Cardinal of England', Henry Beaufort, personally witnessed her terrible death.

Twenty-five years later, in 1456, Joan was formally rehabilitated, and the sentence of excommunication against her was cancelled. Her reputation grew over the centuries, and in 1920 – almost five centuries after her death – she was canonized to become St Joan, the patron saint of France.

Today, Joan's statue is within sight of Cardinal Beaufort's sumptuous tomb, and she is shown looking towards the man who supervised her trial.

On 30 May 1928, the anniversary of Joan's death, a poignant act of reconciliation took place in the cathedral, during which this statue was unveiled in front of many important dignitaries, including the French Ambassador.

Within the hexagonal base of St Joan's statue is a tiny fragment of stone from the dungeon in Rouen where she spent her last agonising days.

Statue of St Joan, looking at Cardinal Beaufort.

HENRY BEAUFORT, 'CARDINAL OF ENGLAND'

Perhaps unfairly, Cardinal Beaufort has become remembered principally for his role as villain in the story of Joan of Arc. Shakespeare shows him on his deathbed, obviously destined for hell. 'So bad a death argues a monstrous life,' says the Earl of Warwick, in *Henry VI* Part II, Act iii, Scene 3, and the King himself remarks,

> Ah, what a sign it is of evil life
> When death's approach is seen so terrible.

Maybe the 'bad Cardinal' himself was penitent, for he asked in his will that 'every day three masses be celebrated for my soul by three monks in the Chapel of my sepulchre. And that the name of Henry Cardinal be pronounced. . . .'

However, when we see this huge and pretentious tomb (the red figure of the Cardinal was added two centuries later, in the reign of Charles II) we must remember Beaufort's generosity in re-founding the Hospital of St Cross, and for beginning the 'Almshouse of Noble Poverty' (*see* pp. 102–5). He also paid for the Great Screen (*see* p. 16), and may have given the City Cross to Winchester (*see* p. 75).

Beaufort was the illegitimate son of John of Gaunt, the half-brother of Henry IV and uncle of Henry V. He was the richest man in England and paid for his nephew's wars in France, including the Battle of Agincourt. He entertained Henry V lavishly at Wolvesey Palace (*see* pp. 98–9) just before the 'warlike Harry' set off for this campaign.

Cardinal Beaufort's impressive memorial.

WILL IT RAIN ON ST SWITHUN'S DAY?

St Swithun's Day, if thou dost rain
For forty days it will remain.
St Swithun's Day, if thou be fair,
The forty days will rain no mair.

This bit of doggerel sums up the famous superstition that if it rains on 15 July – St Swithun's Day – then there will be rain for the next forty days; but if it's sunny, then the sun will shine for the same forty-day period.

The legend has lingered in people's minds for centuries. Today, in the twenty-first century, television weather forecasters still joke about it.

The story goes back to the day St Swithun's remains were dug up – 15 July 971. According to legend, as soon as the spade lifted the first piece of turf on his grave, the heavens opened, rain poured down, and wet weather continued for those famous forty days.

The point is, Swithun – as a gesture of humility – had asked to be buried in ground *outside* the old Saxon minster. The bad weather was a sign of his displeasure at being moved inside, against his expressed wishes.

WHO WAS ST SWITHUN?

It is impossible to exaggerate the importance of St Swithun in Winchester, especially throughout the Middle Ages. Here are the true facts:

· He was Bishop of Winchester at a desperate time, 852–62, when the marauding Danes were attacking England and creating havoc.
· He was the tutor of King Alfred the Great's father, King Ethelwulf, and also of Alfred himself, taking him to Rome to meet the Pope.
· He was responsible for building and repairing many churches; he built the first bridge over the River Itchen in Winchester; he also built a strong wall around the Old Minster, helping to protect the townsfolk against the ferocious invading Danes.
· His shrine in the Saxon cathedral brought thousands of pilgrims to the city, and when the Norman cathedral was built, his bones were transferred there in a newer, even more elaborate shrine. Huge numbers of invalids arrived daily, hoping for a cure to their ailments. For more than half a millennium Winchester resembled modern-day Lourdes.
· The shrine was demolished in 1538 on the orders of Henry VIII. It had to be demolished at night-time to avoid a public outcry.
· In 1962, 1,000 years after Swithun's death, a new shrine was consecrated in his memory (see opposite page).

THE MODERN SHRINE IN MEMORY OF ST SWITHUN

St Swithun's shrine: the 'rainy side' and the 'sunny

This unique shrine was consecrated in 1962 and reminds us of the popular legend about the weather associated with the saint. On the north side the cloth is grey with glass 'raindrops', while the cloth on the south side is a cheerful sunny golden colour. Worked into the metal stand are broken 'eggshells', which refer to the story of the mended eggs (see below).

SWITHUN AND THE MENDED EGGSHELLS

According to local legend, Bishop Swithun performed only one miracle during his lifetime. One day he saw an old woman bringing a basket of eggs to sell in Winchester market. Unfortunately, someone knocked against her and she dropped her basket, breaking the eggs within it. Taking pity on her, Swithun miraculously restored the broken eggs back into their shells! This odd little miracle is remembered both on the Great Screen (*see* p. 16) and on the modern shrine (see above).

After his death, however, St Swithun – as he had then become – was believed to be responsible for thousands of miracles occurring over the following six centuries. An account of Swithun's miracles, recorded by Lantfredus, a tenth-century Winchester monk, tells us that:

> After the body of the most holy bishop was placed within the church, four or five sick persons received cures at his tomb in the space of three days. After the three days, and for about five months there was rarely a day on which sick people were not cured in the church. . . We have seen more than two hundred in ten days cured by the merits of the saint, and in the course of a year, who knows how many?

SIX 'CHANTRIES' AND ONE 'CHAPELL'

Chantries are places within a church built specially for honouring and remembering the important people buried there. They are, in fact, elaborate memorial tombs.

The very name 'chantry' comes from the fact that they were places where there was singing or 'chanting' of a mass for the soul of the person buried there. Of course, only the rich and most powerful could afford to pay for such a luxury after their death.

In 1547 in England, chantries were discontinued and abolished following the dissolution of the monasteries by Henry VIII. However, Winchester Cathedral is exceptionally lucky to possess six of the most beautiful remaining chantries in the country. The plan of the cathedral on pages 2–3 shows where you can find them. They contain the bodies of six of Winchester's most important bishops: William of Edington, William of Wykeham, Cardinal Henry Beaufort, William of Wayneflete, Thomas Langton and Richard Fox. All these chantries exhibit superb decorations, carvings and curious devices.

In fact, there is a seventh – in which Stephen Gardiner is buried. But as he died in 1555, when chantries had officially ceased to exist, his chantry was carefully called a 'chapell'!

Bishop Fox's chantry.

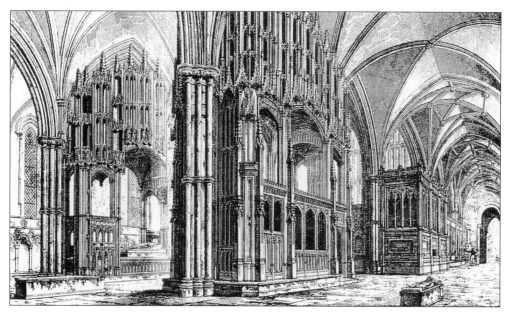

View looking west, roughly from where the statue of St Joan now stands. To the left is the chantry of Cardinal Beaufort, in the middle is the chantry of Bishop Wayneflete and to the right is the 'chapell' of Bishop Stephen Gardiner.

Wood carving in Bishop Langton's chantry.

A STONE CORPSE AND A BLEEDING PELICAN

One of the most beautiful chantries in the cathedral is that of Richard Fox, who was bishop from 1501 to 1528, during the reigns of Henry VII and Henry VIII.

Inside, easily seen through its opening in the south aisle, is a stone carving of a skeleton. This was the age of Holbein's series of woodcuts, *The Dance of Death*, and throughout Europe, artists and sculptors were creating images of skeletons and Death, the Grim Reaper.

Death was shown to be no respecter of rank: the moral was quite simple – the important person here is dead: and one day you too will die.

In his time, Richard Fox was Lord Privy Seal to Henry VII. He baptised Henry VIII and founded Corpus Christi College in Oxford. He also founded schools in Taunton and Grantham.

In Winchester he is remembered for having beautified the cathedral in many ways. He built the stone screen on each side of the quire, on which the six mortuary chests are placed, and he added the fascinating ninety-one coloured bosses of the roof of the quire (*see* pp. 26–9). He also added the flying buttresses on the east end of the cathedral.

Bishop Fox ordered this chantry to be built for himself while he was still alive, in the early years of his time as bishop. Sadly, as an old man he became blind and very frail, and was led to his chantry daily to spend his days in prayer. In his will he asked to be buried here on the day of his death. This was duly done.

. . . AND THE PELICAN?

The curious heraldic device of Bishop Richard Fox is that of a pelican pecking its own breast so that its blood flows down to feed its chicks. In the terminology of heraldry, this image is known as a *pelican in its piety*.

The widely held medieval belief was that by pecking its breast to feed its young, the pelican was an emblem of Jesus Christ, who gave his own blood for the salvation of mankind. (This strange belief may come from the fact that pelicans feed their chicks by transferring macerated food from the bag under their beaks.)

The pelican device of Bishop Fox appears on the pinnacles of his chantry. It is also carved on the Great Screen (*see* pp. 16–17), just below the feet of Christ. Also, Fox's pelicans appear on the cathedral's exterior flying buttresses.

Above: Bishop Fox lying within his chantry.

Bishop Fox's emblem of a 'Pelican in her Piety'. This particular image is drawn from the central boss in the ceiling of his chantry.

ELEVEN HUNDRED BOSSES

Wherever you are in Winchester Cathedral, it is worth looking up at the roof to see the galaxy of carvings at the intersections of ribs in the vaulting – known as 'bosses' (an older name was 'knottes'). It is impossible to describe them all, for there are well over a thousand of them – in the nave; in the quire and retrochoir; in the Lady Chapel; in the aisles; and in the roofs of the tower and the chantries.

Arguably, by far the most interesting of these are the coloured bosses – ninety-one in all – in the quire. These were added in about 1506 by Bishop Fox, who did so much to beautify the cathedral during his period in office (1501–28).

These quire bosses are wooden and are bolted on to the roof, covering smaller, less elaborate bosses which were already there. From east to west, they fall into three groups. First (over the altar) come thirty symbols and images of the Passion of Jesus Christ; secondly, there are bosses containing royal coats of arms and references to Tudor royalty; and thirdly, there are the arms of Bishop Fox himself (the pelican again) and arms relating to the various other cathedrals where he had held office (Exeter, Bath and Wells, and Durham).

It is worth bringing binoculars to see the bosses more clearly, but they are fairly easy to identify without such help. They run in three rows – and here are the Passion symbols, running from east to west in each row:

NORTH ROW (LEFT)		CENTRAL ROW		SOUTH ROW (RIGHT)
I	Head of spitting Jew (*Matt. xxvi,* 67)	I	A pelican (*see* pp. 24–5)	I Hand holding Jesus's hair (*Isaiah l,* 6)
II	A smiting hand (*Matt. xxvi,* 67)	II	Chalice of the Agony in the Garden (*Matt. xxvi,* 42)	II Head of High Priest (*Matt. xxvi,* 3)
III	Three nails with an intertwining cord	III	The Cross, with three nails	III Spear, sponge on a reed, and loincloth
IV	A basin and ewer (*Matt. xxvii,* 24)	IV	Cross, with bleeding heart, hands and feet (*see* opposite page)	IV Jesus and Judas (the Betrayal) (*Matt. xxvi,* 48–49)
V	Judas' moneybag and 30 pieces of silver (*Matt. xxvii,* 3)	V	Face of Jesus on St Veronica's handkerchief	V A crowing cockerel (Matt. xxvi, 74)
VI	Lantern with candle (*John xviii,* 3)	VI	Hammer and pair of pincers	VI Torch and brazier (*John xviii,* 3)
VII	Three dice (*John, xix,* 24) (*see* opposite page)	VII	Pillar of the Flagellation and two scourges	VII Pestle and mortar (for wine mixed with myrrh)
		VIII	Ladder	
		IX	Another pelican	

The series continues with royal emblems and then with Bishop Fox's emblems, but there are other passion emblems over the north-east and south-east windows.

THE PASSION STORY TOLD AMONG THE BOSSES

Cross with five wounds; hands, feet and heart surmounted with the crown of thorns.

The dice used by the soldiers to cast lots for Jesus's clothes. (*Matt, xxvii*, 35)

Malchus, the High Priest's servant, with his ear being cut off by a sword. (*John, xviii*, 10)

MORE CURIOUS BOSSES

Obviously, it's impossible to mention all the 1,100-plus bosses in the cathedral, but you may be interested to find these bosses, which are especially intriguing:

QUIRE – following on from the series devoted to the emblems of the Passion:
Royal Series:
Three crowns – possibly the mythical arms of St Edmund, King and Martyr
Cross with four birds – emblem of the Saxon kings of England
Fleur-de-lis of France
Royal arms, surmounted with the Garter and with a crown
H & K – referring to Henry VIII and Katherine of Aragon
Royal coat of arms with the red dragon of Wales and the white greyhound of the
  House of Beaufort
Crowned hawthorn bush with the letters H R – the monogram of Henry VII
White hart – emblem of Richard II
White antelope – emblem of Henry IV
A tree stump with roots – a 'rebus' (see p. 44) referring to the former Royal Manor
  of Woodstock (now destroyed)

Bishop Fox Series
These are understood when we remember that a bishop's arms consist of the arms
  of his diocese on the left side as we look at the shield, and his personal arms on
  the right. Thus, Bishop Fox's shields are as follows:
Bishop of Exeter – upright sword with keys and pelican
Bishop of Bath and Wells – St Andrew's cross and pelican
Bishop of Durham – four lions and pelican
Bishop of Winchester – keys and sword (see p. 1) and pelican

SOUTH AISLE OF NAVE:
Sow suckling her three piglets, being carried off by a lion
'Green Man' (*see* opposite page)
Adam and Eve
Man playing a double pipe
Angel carrying a shield displaying the Prince of Wales' feathers
Two monks holding a book, with a fox between them
Bird and three fledglings on a nest
Man baiting a bull with a dog
Angel playing a citole (an early medieval stringed instrument)

NORTH AISLE OF NAVE:
Man playing bagpipes
Arms of the Saxon kings of England (see opposite page)

There are many more to be found throughout the cathedral – so please make your
own discoveries!

The Green Man.

The supposed arms of the Saxon kings showing martlets – traditionally shown without feet or legs.

A grotesque figure lurking in the shadows.

THIRTEEN OBJECTS FOUND IN THE 'RUFUS TOMB'. . . BUT WHOSE TOMB WAS IT?

The great Norman tomb in the middle of the quire stalls was formerly believed to contain the remains of the wicked William Rufus, son of William the Conqueror. However, experts now think it more likely to be the tomb of Bishop Henry of Blois, grandson of the Conqueror.

The massive Norman tomb was opened up in 1868. Inside, investigators found the bones of a skeleton which had been disturbed – possibly during the time of Oliver Cromwell. Intriguingly, thirteen other items were also found inside the tomb, some of which can now be seen on display near the cathedral library.

Most investigators at the time were convinced that the tomb was indeed that of Rufus. However, others thought differently, especially as one of the mortuary chests (see pp. 32–3) is marked as containing Rufus's bones. Whatever the truth about the bones, here are the other objects found among them:

1. Fragments of a lead coffin 2. Cloth of gold 3. Red cloth 4. Seven gold braids of Norman pattern 5. Three kinds of muslin 6. Remains of cloth lining to the lead coffin 7. Other fabrics resembling serges 8. A turquoise
9. An ivory griffin's head 10. Fragments of small wands 11. Some flat pieces of cork 12. Some broken nutshells, small twigs and pieces of bark
13. Remains of a weapon

The shape of this massive Norman tomb in the choir is known as 'dos d'âne', or 'back of a donkey'! For many years it was known as the 'Rufus Tomb', but it is now thought to be that of Bishop Henry of Blois (d. 1171). (*John Crook*)

FACTS AND LEGENDS ABOUT RUFUS, 'THE RED KING'

On 2 August 1100 William 'Rufus', known as the 'Red King' because of his red hair and ruddy complexion, was killed by an arrow in the New Forest. The most likely suspect was Sir Walter Tyrell, a member of the Red King's hunting party on that day. Tyrell fled the country immediately after the killing, never to return.

It was certainly a mysterious death. No one will ever know whether it was an accident or a deliberately planned murder. The king's body was found by a charcoal burner named Purkis, who put the bleeding corpse on his cart and trundled it all the way to Winchester Cathedral, 20 miles away. There, the horrified monks shovelled the body into a grave beneath the cathedral's tower, without any proper Christian rites. They hated Rufus, who scoffed at their religion, and was vindictive, avaricious and homosexual.

The 'Rufus Stone' in the New Forest, traditionally marking the spot where William II (Rufus) was killed in 1100. (*Mary Hilliam*)

Seven years later, the tower of the cathedral collapsed. The monks were convinced that the presence of the Red King's evil corpse was to blame.

LEGENDS

Ocknell Pond, near the scene of the murder, is supposed to turn red on the anniversary of the king's death. It is where Tyrell washed the blood from his guilty hands.

The blacksmith at a nearby village put horseshoes backwards on Tyrell's horse, to confuse any pursuers. Well into the nineteenth century, a fine of £3 10s was paid to the crown by the Lord Lieutenant of Hampshire as a penalty for this crime. Purkis, the charcoal burner, asked Henry I for the right of felling timber in the New Forest as a reward. The king gave Purkis the right to collect any boughs he could reach with a woodman's hook and crook; hence the expression, 'by hook or by crook'.

Plaque on a wall of the Town Hall, Romsey.

A strange theory was put forward that the death of Rufus was linked to a pre-Christian pagan ritual killing. The event happened on the 'morrow of Lammas' – which was one of the four witch-festivals of the year: (Hallowe'en, Candlemas, Walpurgis Night, and Lammas). Perhaps Rufus knew he would be killed.

A huge black hairy he-goat was seen on the day of the murder. When questioned, the goat confessed that he was the Devil, on his way to take the Red King to Hell.

SIX BOXES OF ROYAL BONES

Close to the Great Screen, on each side of the presbytery, are beautifully carved stone screens given to the cathedral by Bishop Fox. On top of these screens are six wooden mortuary chests – three on each side.

These unique chests contain the mortal remains of some of the earliest Saxon kings. They are the oldest royal bones in England. Westminster Abbey has nothing as old as these. These kingly bones, together with the remains of some Saxon bishops, belonged to:

KING CYNEGILS (reigned 611–43), the first Christian king of Wessex
KING CENWALH (reigned 643–72), Cynegils' son, who first built a minster here
KING EGBERT (reigned 802–39), the first overlord of all the Saxon kingdoms
KING ETHELWULF (reigned 839–59), father of King Alfred the Great
KING CANUTE (CNUT) (reigned 1016–35), Danish king of England
QUEEN EMMA (died 1052), wife of King Ethelred the Unready and, later, wife of
    King Canute (often spelt Cnut)

BISHOP WINE (662–3), who consecrated Saint Chad
BISHOP ALWINE (1032–47), friend of Queen Emma
BISHOP STIGAND (1047–70), last Saxon Bishop of Winchester and last Saxon
    Archbishop of Canterbury

Unfortunately, no one knows exactly who lies in which chest! In 1642, Cromwell's Parliamentarian soldiers broke open the chests and tipped the contents onto the cathedral floor. They then used the bigger bones to throw at the stained-glass windows to smash them. An inscription on one of the chests tells how the contents got jumbled up as they were later put back:

In this chest, in 1661, were promiscuously laid the bones of princes and prelates which had been scattered by sacrilegious barbarism in 1642.

These jumbled bones are the oldest royal remains in England. Mixed up here may be the bones of Saxon kings: Egbert, Ethelwulf and Edmund I – but no one will ever know exactly who is who. (*John Crook*)

One of the three mortuary chests on the north side of the choir. They rest on the stone screen made during the bishopric of Richard Fox, 1500–29. (*John Crook*)

A drawing of the inner chest which may contain the bones of King Cynegils (611–43), who founded Winchester's first cathedral in 641, and also the bones of King Ethelwulf (who reigned between 839 and 858).

THE ASTONISHING STORY OF QUEEN EMMA

In one of the mortuary chests are the remains of Queen Emma, one of the great characters of her time. She had the unique distinction of marrying two kings of England (Ethelred and Canute), and being the mother of two other kings of England (Hardecanute and Edward the Confessor).

In her younger days, she was said to be remarkably beautiful and was known as the 'Fair Maid', but as she grew older, she gained a reputation for wisdom and was known as the 'Old Lady'. She was the Queen Mother of her time.

The most astonishing episode in her long and eventful life is totally apocryphal, but, like the tale of Alfred and the burnt cakes, it's a story with a life of its own and deserves to be preserved as a part of English folklore.

According to the medieval chronicler, Richard of Devizes, Emma was accused in her second widowhood of having an affair with Alwine, Bishop of Winchester. By then, her son Edward the Confessor was on the throne, and he ordered that Emma should undergo a terrifying form of trial by ordeal.

Within the nave of Winchester's Old Minster, nine ploughshares were to be heated to become red-hot and Emma was required to walk upon them with bare feet. If her feet were burnt, she would be proved guilty, but if she came through the ordeal unscathed, she would be shown to be innocent.

The old chronicler tells how Emma spent the previous night beside the tomb of St Swithun, praying for help, and in a dream, heard the voice of the saint telling her not to be afraid.

The next day, in full view of her son the king and a great congregation of onlookers, Emma took off her shoes and, guided by two bishops, trod on each of the nine sharp and red-hot ploughshares – and when she had completed the ordeal, her feet were found to be perfectly untouched and without blemish. She was innocent!

She was so delighted that she gave nine manor houses to the monks of Old Minster, and Bishop Alwine, who, of course, was also proved to be innocent, gave nine more – one for each of the red-hot ploughshares.

In today's cathedral, Emma's bones lie in a mortuary chest, probably mingled with those of her second husband, Canute, and with those of her friend, the bishop.

MEMORIES OF 'OLD MINSTER'

The former Saxon cathedral was known as 'Old Minster'. Ruthlessly, the Normans demolished it as soon as they had completed their own cathedral – the one we know today. However, over the centuries, people completely forgot where Old Minster was in relation to the Norman building.

In the 1960s, after several years of extensive archaeological digs, the outlines of Old Minster were revealed, and although we can only guess what the Saxon cathedral actually looked like, at least we now know the outline of its foundations. Today, this outline is marked on the lawn just to the north of the cathedral (to the left as you look at the West Front). The best view is from the cathedral roof, though unfortunately, this is rarely possible.

A fine white ledger stone, inscribed with the word SWITHUN, marks the spot where the saint's original grave lay. St Swithun's remains had been removed from this grave in 971 to be placed

The outline of the former Saxon cathedral, 'Old Minster', as seen from the present cathedral roof. (*John Crook*)

within a shrine inside Old Minster. Arguably, this was the most important event ever to take place there. But as we regard this grassy piece of turf, we should remember that this is the site of other events which have taken place here, when Old Minster stood here in all its glory.

According to the *Anglo-Saxon Chronicle*, King Cenwalh built the first church here in 648 – and hazy tradition has it that he built it on the site of a much earlier church, built in Roman times, in the year 164. Be that as it may, the following events certainly took place somewhere on this site:

Many of the earliest Saxon kings and saints were buried here:

It was the first burial place of King Alfred the Great, in 899.
King Canute was crowned here in about 1017.
Edward the Confessor was crowned here in 1042.
Matilda, wife of William the Conqueror, was crowned here in 1068.

MONKS AND MOMENTS OF HIGH DRAMA

One of Winchester's most influential Saxon bishops – sadly, almost forgotten today – was St Aethelwold. During his nineteen years of office (963–82) he transformed the cathedral by enlarging it greatly and turning it into a Benedictine monastery.

The moment of change was charged with surprise and high drama, taking place in Old Minster.

One Sunday at the beginning of Lent, Aethelwold peremptorily ordered all the married canons of the cathedral to put on hooded garments and become celibate monks. Despite their vigorous protests, Aethelwold turned them all out – except three – and then triumphantly produced a party of monks from Abingdon Abbey, who had been waiting outside ready to enter Old Minster and take their place.

The ejected canons were furious and appealed to King Edgar himself, who called a Witan (parliament) to discuss the matter, and Archbishop Dunstan came to Winchester to support Aethelwold.

The debate was wavering, until a spine-tingling moment came. Suddenly, a powerful voice came from a crucifix hanging against the wall! It urged them not to hesitate any longer, but to support the creation of monks forthwith!

After such divine intervention, this Benedictine monastery with all its monks lasted for almost 600 years.

THE GREAT ORGAN OF OLD MINSTER

Many precious items were held in Old Minster – but probably the most remarkable object was an early version of a pipe organ, built under the direction of St Aethelwold. It was a gigantic contraption – with no fewer than 400 pipes worked by twenty-six bellows, and pumped by seventy strong men who worked like galley slaves, with toil and sweat. Wulfstan, a tenth-century monk of St Swithun's Abbey, ecstatically described this amazing organ in Latin verse. Translated, it reads:

Two brethren play the organ . . . and when the players pushed in these tongues [keys] and set free the sound, forth issued seven jubilant notes. Like thunder the iron voice assaults the ears and drives out every other sound. Nay, so swells the sound that as you hear you must clap your hands to your ears, unable as you draw near to abide the brazen bellowing. All through the city the melody can be heard: and the fame and the echo spread through all lands.

It has been claimed that at the time it was built, Aethelwold's great instrument was probably the most complicated piece of machinery in the world!

ST SWITHUN'S ARM – TAKEN TO NORWAY BY A TWELFTH-CENTURY MONK

The fame of St Swithun spread far and wide throughout medieval Europe. This was a time when there was a huge respect for holy relics, and parts of saints' bodies were often solemnly taken from their graves and transferred to other shrines elsewhere. Bones, skulls, arms, legs, toes, fingers: bishops and priests everywhere were keen to possess relics for their cathedrals and churches.

In the early twelfth century Reinhald, a Winchester monk, travelled to Norway, taking Swithun's right arm with him as a relic to place in a newly-built cathedral, dedicated to St Swithun and consecrated in 1125 at Stavanger.

This link between Winchester and Stavanger was celebrated in 1971, to mark 1,000 years since Swithun's remains were reburied in Old Minster (see pp. 20–1). The city of Stavanger presented the Dean and Chapter of Winchester with the white ledger stone, which now marks the exact spot where Swithun had originally been buried – *outside* Old Minster in 862. The ledger stone was placed in position exactly 1,000 years to the day since that momentous occasion when the rains began to fall!

The memorial stone can be seen on the north side of the cathedral, from the railings by the West Front, though it is unfortunately not possible to get close to it.

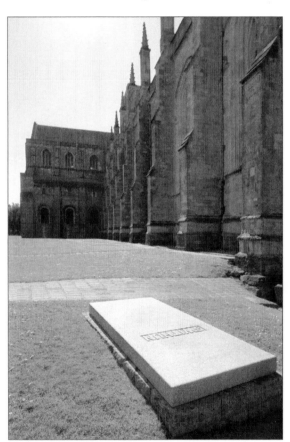

The stone by the north side of the cathedral marking the original grave of St Swithun. (*John Crook*)

'THAT BUGGER AIN'T BILL!'
THE STORY OF THE WINCHESTER DIVER

The story of how Winchester Cathedral was saved from collapse by the extraordinary work of William Walker – or 'Diver Bill' as he has been called – has virtually passed into folklore.

In the early years of the twentieth century, Winchester Cathedral was in serious danger of falling down. Its foundations had been built on a timber raft lying on a bed of peat. Over the centuries, compression of this peat had allowed the fabric of the cathedral to sink and crack. Much remedial work had become necessary.

The best solution was to send a diver down to lay sacks of cement and underpin the sagging walls. It was an immense task. William Walker, the diver chosen to undertake the job, went down into the filthy, dark, cold waters beneath the cathedral almost daily for six years, from 1906 to 1912, placing bags of cement to shore up the sinking walls. Of course, there was a large support team above him, but during those years, Walker single-handedly placed 25,800 bags of concrete into position, together with 114,900 concrete blocks and 900,000 bricks.

King George V, Queen Mary, and a large number of dignitaries attended a thanksgiving service in 1912, to celebrate the saving of the cathedral, and the King shook William Walker's hand, congratulating him on his achievement.

Half a century later, Sir Charles Wheeler was commissioned to make a statuette to commemorate William Walker, and in March 1964, in the south east corner of the cathedral, this was unveiled. Horror of horrors! Wheeler had been given a somewhat indistinct photograph from which to model the likeness, and he had accidentally omitted to adorn Bill with his distinctive walrus moustache! The diver's face was clean-shaven! Members of Walker's family were dumbfounded, and one of them was heard to exclaim, 'That bugger ain't Bill!'

The first – clean-shaven – statue of 'Diver Bill'. This statue remained in the cathedral for many years.

It was extremely embarrassing, and at first, the situation was hushed up for fear of offending the donor who had paid for it. To rectify matters, a second statue was put up by Norman Pierce, a local sculptor. It stands near the entrance to the cathedral shop and it shows the real William Walker, with his generously proportioned walrus moustache. The discrepancy between the two statues was still apparent though, so in 2001 a third statue was made, this time by Professor Glyn Williams, to replace the first one which had stood on its plinth, wrongly depicting Walker for thirty-seven years. Today, visitors can enjoy two statues, both inside and outside the cathedral, and both giving a true likeness of Diver Bill.

The 'proper' statue of 'Diver Bill', by Norman Pierce This can be seen in the garden just outside the present refectory.

This bust of William Walker by Professor Glyn Williams can now be seen at the east end of the cathedral.

WILLIAM OF WYKEHAM'S CHANTRY
... BUT WHO ARE THE THREE LITTLE MEN?

William of Wykeham came from humble parents and rose to become immensely powerful through sheer ability and ferocious energy. For many years he was the richest and most powerful man in the country. The contemporary French historian, Jean Froissart, wrote that 'Sir William de Wican reigned in England . . . By him everything was done and without him they did nothing.'

William was born in the Hampshire village of Wickham, about 15 miles south-east of Winchester, perhaps the son of a peasant. He must have been a bright youngster, attracting the notice of Nicholas Uvedale, lord of the manor at Wickham, who sent young William to the Prior's school in Winchester. With this generous help, William's career advanced astonishingly swiftly.

His first job was as secretary to the constable of Winchester Castle (see pp. 58–9); then he became clerk to the Sheriff of Hampshire; then he joined Edward III's service as Chief Warden and Surveyor of royal castles, including Windsor and Dover. The King soon appointed him his Private Secretary and Keeper of the Privy Seal, and finally, in 1367, he became Chancellor.

During this meteoric rise to power, the King heaped immense riches on Wykeham, giving him prebends (share in the revenue) of St Paul's London, Hereford, Salisbury, St David's, Beverley, Lincoln, York and Wells. In addition to being Chancellor of England, he was also appointed Bishop of Winchester.

It is impossible to exaggerate his power, wealth, or the legacy which he has left – in at least three memorable ways: first, the founding of Winchester College, which became the model for English public schools; secondly, the founding of New College, Oxford; and thirdly (aged 70!) as Bishop of Winchester, he funded and personally oversaw the transformation of the cathedral (see p. 6).

This is the man whose effigy lies so peacefully in this chantry, with three lifelike little figures of men with hands together in prayer, sitting at his feet. But who are they?

Three little figures at the foot of William of Wykeham's tomb. They are possibly Wykeham's close assistants and friends: Nicholas Wykeham, John Elmere and John De Campedene.

WYKEHAM'S FAVOURITE PLACE TO PRAY

William of Wykeham's chantry, with his effigy within, is situated in the bay between two pillars in the south aisle. As a young teenager, this was Wykeham's favourite place in the cathedral where he would come to pray. It is especially fitting that his tomb is placed here.

Tradition has it that when Cromwell's soldiers entered the cathedral on their rampage in 1642, Nicholas Fiennes, one of Cromwell's generals but also a member of the Wykeham family and a former Wykehamist, placed himself at the entrance to this chantry and sternly forbade anyone to enter or do any harm to it.

William of Wykeham's chantry in the south aisle.

William of Wykeham's tomb within the chantry. Wykeham designed this for himself.

A BISHOP'S CARVED SKELETON SMASHED BY CROMWELL'S TROOPS

Bishop Stephen Gardiner was a steadfast Catholic during the turbulent times of the sixteenth century. When the fanatically Protestant young king Edward VI, aged 9, came to the throne, he ordered Bishop Gardiner to preach before him so that he could judge the bishop's theological soundness. Gardiner went through the ordeal thinking that he had done so without offence. Alarmingly, the very next day he was arrested, deprived of his bishopric, and sent to the Tower of London. Here, he was kept prisoner for the next five years.

His fortune changed when the Catholic Mary Tudor came to the throne. One of her first acts on entering London was to go directly to the Tower of London and to release him, together with other high profile captives imprisoned for their beliefs. Mary is said to have burst into tears as she recognised old friends kneeling before her. 'Ye are *my* prisoners!' she said; and raised them one by one, kissed them and gave them their liberty.

Just three months later, Stephen Gardiner, now restored to dignity and office, had the honour of crowning Mary in Westminster Abbey. The task should have been given to the Archbishop of Canterbury, Thomas Cranmer, but at that time, it was his turn to be imprisoned in the Tower.

Then, shortly after, it was Bishop Stephen Gardiner who married Queen Mary and Philip of Spain in Winchester Cathedral.

Gardiner supported Mary in her attempt to turn England back to Catholicism, except that he withdrew from involvement in the terrible persecutions and burnings: for this, he is to be honoured. Nevertheless, memories of that time were still sharp almost a century later. His carved memorial skeleton within this chantry, in the south aisle, was smashed in two by the Parliamentarian troops. It was a time of sectarian hate. Even in death, Gardiner was still reviled.

Stephen Gardiner's cadaver cracked in two within its chantry (tactfully called a 'chapell').

WINCHESTER CATHEDRAL IS ABOLISHED – BY LAW!

During the Civil War and the period of the Commonwealth which followed, Winchester Cathedral suffered ruthless vandalism by Puritan troops who captured the city. A contemporary writer, calling himself Mercurius Rusticus, describes how,

> . . . on Tuesday the 12 of December 1642 [the rebels] entered the City that afternoon between two and three; being Masters of the City, they instantly fall upon the Close . . . they seize the Prebends Horses, and demand their Persons with many threatening words . . . on Thursday morning between nine, and ten of the Clock . . . they violently break open the Cathedral Church, and . . . enter the Church with Colours flying, their drums beating, their Matches fired . . . until they came to the Altar . . . and burnt the Books of Common Prayer, and all the Singing Books belonging to the Quire.

Shortly after this, the Dean and Chapter, were, by law, 'utterly abolished' – in other words, officially the cathedral simply ceased to exist.

The breaking of Bishop Gardiner's skeleton effigy was only one of many acts of vandalism. The troops stabled their horses in the nave of the cathedral; they broke up all the statues on the Great Screen and in niches of the chantries; they destroyed manuscripts and books in the cathedral archives – giving the leaves of some of the precious books to local shopkeepers for use as wrapping paper.

Further, they tipped out all the bones of the Saxon kings from the mortuary chests, and used them up to smash the stained-glass windows.

CHARLES I PASSES THROUGH WINCHESTER ON HIS WAY TO BE EXECUTED

Of course, Charles didn't realise he was going to his death – but in December 1648 he was brought to Winchester on his way to be tried in London. He had been held prisoner in Carisbrooke Castle on the Isle of Wight, and then briefly at Hurst Castle, on the Hampshire coast.

The Civil War had split the country but Winchester was mainly Royalist – so at the arrival of the king, the Mayor and Corporation turned out in state to do him honour – even though he was a prisoner. They presented him with the keys of the city, and on this occasion it is reported that Charles cured a man in the crowd, touching him for the 'King's Evil'.

But the mayor paid the price for his loyalty. Immediately afterwards, the Cromwellian guards set upon him and gave him a severe beating up.

Charles spent just one night here in Winchester, before being hustled on to London. He had just one more month to live.

BISHOP LANGTON'S RIDDLING REBUS

'Rebus' is Latin for 'with things'. In earlier centuries, when most people couldn't read, the names of persons or places were sometimes depicted by means of 'things' – pictures or carvings of objects that, if said aloud, resembled the sound of that name.

Some of these were extraordinary three-dimensional puns, requiring an odd kind of ingenuity to work them out. Shown below is a splendid example of just how tortuous some of these medieval rebuses could be. It refers to the name of Thomas Langton, who was Bishop of Winchester from 1493 to 1501. His chantry is in the north-east corner of the cathedral – a separate chapel decorated with elaborate carvings of great beauty. This rebus is to be found several times on bosses within this chantry.

To understand this, we must recognise the capital 'T' for Thomas. This is resting on a barrel or 'tun'. Then there is a long lower case letter 'l' passing vertically through both the 'T' and the tun. Somewhat tortuously, we can read this as the name of 'Thomas Lang (long) – tun'. The letter 'l' has sometimes been interpreted as being a 'long' note in the musical notation of that time.

Thomas Langton's rebus.

PRIOR SILKSTEDE'S EASY REBUS

One of the most beautiful objects in the cathedral is 'Prior Silkstede's Pulpit', which is to be found in the quire. Prior Sillkstede (1498–1524) was one of the last priors of the Abbey of St Swithun's (i.e. the present cathedral).

The pulpit is well worth close inspection. The wood carving shows skeins of silk, both on the pulpit itself and on the rails of its elaborate twisting staircase. No one can see this rebus without thinking of Prior Silkstede, who paid for it to be made.

Prior Silkstede's pulpit, decorated with skeins of silk.

PRIORS AND BISHOPS

The position of 'Prior' is perhaps unfamiliar to modern visitors. It should be remembered that throughout the Middle Ages, the cathedral was first and foremost the abbey church of a monastery – a busy community of monks who lived in a large complex of buildings in the Close (*see* pp. 48–9). The head of this community was the Prior, who ruled over every aspect of the monks' lives.

The office 'Bishop' is quite separate. Although a bishop had the right to visit his cathedral (*cathedra* = 'a seat' – i.e. the seat of a bishop), in actual fact, his authority there was subservient to that of the Prior. At the Reformation, after English monasteries were abolished, the 'Dean' headed the ruling body of Winchester Cathedral. In 1541, the last Prior of St Swithun's Abbey became the first Dean of Winchester Cathedral – but of course, the monks had been forced to go. In brief, a dean is in charge of the cathedral, while a bishop is in charge of the diocese.

AN EIGHTEENTH-CENTURY HEADMASTER
TEACHING HIS BOYS

Against the wall of the south aisle are two memorial sculptures by the great artist John Flaxman (1755–1826). One of these is an elegant and fascinating scene showing Dr Joseph Warton (1722–1800), poet, literary critic and Headmaster of Winchester College.

Joseph Warton's memorial.

He is depicted teaching a group of pupils standing in front of him while he sits with a book in his hand. Beautifully designed, it gives us a memorable view of eighteenth-century Winchester schoolboys. The contemporary clothes of the boys and Dr Warton's wig are details to be enjoyed. The other Flaxman memorial is that of Henrietta Maria North.

Discipline in Winchester College during Dr Warton's headmastership was somewhat lax, and there were several instances of schoolboys' mutinies, the worst of which took place in 1783 and was known as 'The Great Rebellion'. As a result of this, about thirty-five pupils were expelled, and shortly afterwards Dr Warton himself decided to retire. However, boys usually behaved themselves – being warned in Latin of the consequences of laxness on a board displayed in the school; *AUT DISCE AUT DISCEDE, MANET SORS TERTIA, CAEDI* – which means: 'Either you learn, or you get out – the third alternative is to be beaten.' More succinctly: 'Learn, leave or be licked.'

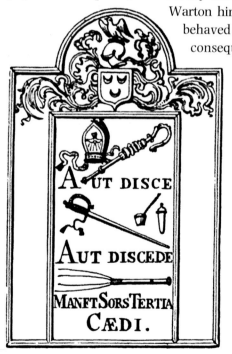

Note that above 'AUT DISCE' is a mitre and crozier – the rewards of learning; above 'Aut discede' is a sword and an inkhorn – the signs of the army and the legal profession; and above the third alternative is a 'bibling-rod' – made from four apple-twigs attached to a handle – which was traditionally used to flog lazy or unruly students.

ISAAK WALTON AND THE FISHERMEN'S WINDOW

Izaak Walton (1593–1683) is buried in the Silkstede Chapel, situated in the south-east corner of the south transept. He is commemorated there with a beautiful and curious stained-glass window, given by the fishermen of England and America. It was placed there in 1914, just before the outbreak of the First World War.

Walton began life as an ironmonger's assistant and a draper, but he became a close friend of John Donne, poet and Dean of St Paul's, London, and through Donne he met Henry King, George Herbert and many other literary churchmen. He became steward of Bishop Morley in Worcester, and came with him when Morley was appointed Bishop of Winchester. He wrote the 'Lives' of Donne, Hooker, Herbert, Sanderson and Sir Henry Wotton. However, Walton's international fame comes from *The Compleat Angler* – a unique work which has been reprinted many hundreds of times.

In the stained-glass window Walton is depicted twice: in one he is by the River Itchen, with St Catherine's Hill in the background: in the other he is shown in Dovedale. Below him is his favourite text, STUDY TO BE QUIET, which comes from 1 Thessalonians, iv, II.

There are many other intriguing 'fishy' details in this window: for example, St Antony of Padua (1195–1231), a friend of St Francis, is shown preaching to the fishes of the

Izaak Walton and the Fishermen's window.

sea. The fish are seen listening to St Antony with their heads popping out of the water. The apostles Peter and Andrew – both fishermen – are also shown. And at the top the Lord is seen as he 'sitteth upon the water flood.'

Walton became the son-in-law of Dr Hawkins, a prebend (canon) of Winchester Cathedral. He lived to be 90, and spent his final years at No. 7 Dome Alley in the Close (*see* plan on the following pages).

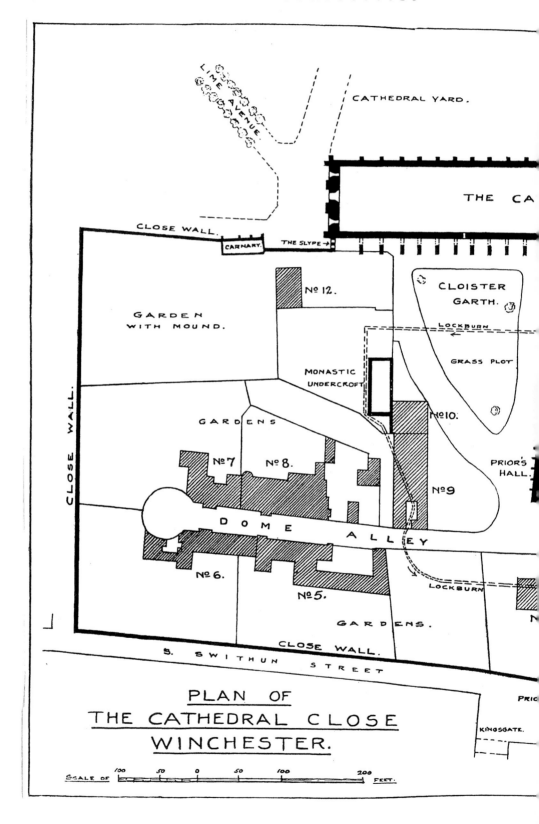

CATHEDRAL YARD.

THE CA

CLOISTER
GARTH.

LINE AVENUE

CLOSE WALL.

CARNARY.

THE SLYPE →

GRASS PLOT

Nº 12.

GARDEN
WITH MOUND.

LOCKBURN

MONASTIC
UNDERCROFT

CLOSE WALL.

GARDENS

Nº 10.

Nº 7

Nº 8.

Nº 9

PRIOR'S
HALL.

DOME   ALLEY

Nº 6.

Nº 5.

LOCKBURN

GARDENS.

CLOSE WALL.

S. SWITHUN   STREET

PRIO

PLAN   OF
THE CATHEDRAL   CLOSE
WINCHESTER.

KINGSGATE.

SCALE OF   100   50   0   50   100   200   FEET.

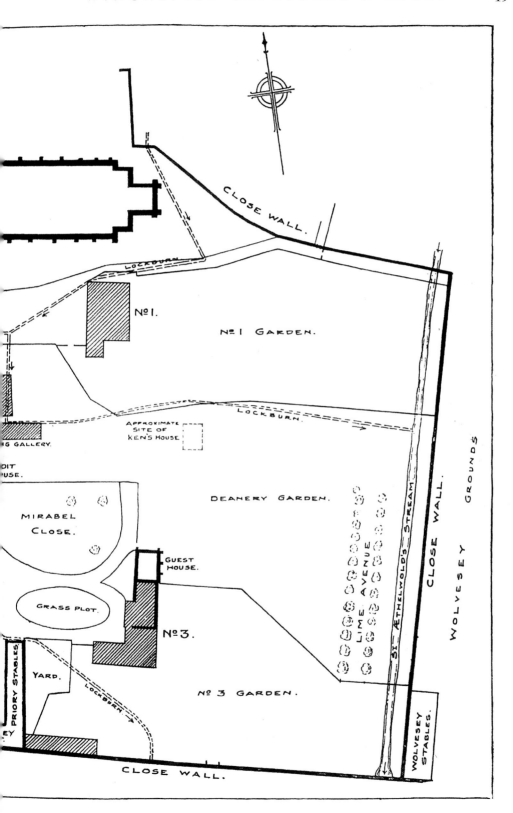

A PAIR OF LATIN PUZZLES TO SOLVE

There's a curious Latin inscription carved on the south corner of the West Front, just where the path leads into the Close. The words are laid out in an odd way, and there are two hands pointing in opposite directions. Roughly translated, the Latin words mean:

WALK THAT WAY IF YOU WANT TO PRAY

WALK THIS WAY IF YOU WANT TO GO THROUGH

The top hand points to the entrance into the cathedral, and the bottom hand points to the passageway into the Close. To solve this odd puzzle, you have to zigzag up and down to work out the meaning. Fully expanded, the Latin reads:

ILLAC PRECATOR . . .
HAC VIATOR . . .   . . . AMBULA

The point about these curiously carved directions is that until the early seventeenth century, there was no passageway here into the Close, and people had to use the cathedral as a thoroughfare, entering by the west door and going up the nave or south aisle, and then out through the south transept.

Bishop Curle, who was bishop between 1632 and 1647, made a number of changes to the cathedral, and it was under his direction that the passage to the south of the cathedral (known as 'The Slype') was opened up. The Latin inscription is a polite reminder not to use the cathedral as a public thoroughfare.

A similar, but more complicated inscription can be found built into the wall on the south side of the 'slype', just after the second buttress. There is the same eccentric patterning of letters and words, but it's not easy to decipher, as the letters are rather worn.

In this carving, a Latin sentence just below the date 1632 reads:

CESSIT COMMUNI PROPRIUM
JAM PERGITE QUA FAS

Meaning 'Private property has given way to public use. Go the way which is now opened up for you'.

Underneath this come the riddling pair of sentences:

SACRA SIT ILLA CHORO, SERVA SIT ISTA FORO

'Let that way be consecrated to the choir. Let this way be used for the market'.

ACR	S	ILL	CH
S	A	IT	A	ORO
ERV	S	IST	F

THE OLD CHAPTER HOUSE

As you enter the Close, notice the site of the old Chapter House, destroyed quite unnecessarily by Bishop Horne in the late sixteenth century. It looks peaceful now, but it was the scene of drama in 1213 when King John came here to be absolved by Archbishop Stephen Langton after having been excommunicated for over a year.

Looking from the Close into what was once the Old Chapter House. It has been thought that the large monolith columns may have been part of some ancient Roman building.

THE DEANERY

One of the oldest buildings in the Close is the Deanery, which was formerly the Prior's Hall. Three pointed arches lead into the small covered porch known as the Pilgrims' Cloister – so-called because from there the pilgrims visiting St Swithun's shrine used to be given leftover food from the Prior's table. It is not possible to visit the Deanery, but you may walk up to these arches and notice the Roman pavement. This pavement was discovered on the site of the flying buttresses when these were erected in the early twentieth century against the south wall of the nave to strengthen it. The Roman pavement in the Deanery is probably the only one in Britain on which people may still walk.

There are royal links to the Deanery: Philip of Spain stayed here in 1554 when he came to marry Mary Tudor; Charles II came here in 1666, bringing his court

(and Nell Gwynn) to avoid the Plague of London; and Queen Elizabeth II gave audience to her Prime Minister, Anthony Eden, here in July 1955.

The Deanery.

DOME ALLEY

Walking south from the Deanery and looking to your right, you will see a short row of red-brick houses named Dome Alley. These houses were built after the Restoration in 1660, but it is interesting to see that the water pipes are Tudor, and are decorated with Tudor roses – evidently taken from some previous buildings. It was at No. 7 Dome Alley that Izaak Walton lived and died in 1683.

Dome Alley, which gets its name from the Latin *domus* meaning 'home'. Its houses were homes for clergy.

THE PILGRIMS' HALL (GUEST HALL)

At the far end of the west side of the Close is a twentieth-century building – part of the Pilgrims' School, and at the left end of this, adjoining it, is a much older building known as the Guest Hall. This is where medieval pilgrims to St Swithun's shrine were given accommodation. It is possible sometimes to look into this and enjoy the wonderful timber roof with massive hammer-beams, some with carved heads. Nowadays it has a small stage, and is part of the preparatory school.

Exterior and interior views of Pilgrims' Guest Hall.

THE PRIORY STABLES

It is well worth looking into the courtyard to the right of the modern part of the Pilgrims' School to get a glimpse of the attractive building which once formed the priory stables. This also now belongs to the Pilgrims' School. Until recently there was an old pump, which drew water from the 'Lockbourne' – the artificially made stream which was created, tradition says, by St Athelwold, to serve the monastic buildings of the Close. The Lockbourne itself is now hidden, running beneath the ground – but its course can be seen marked on the map on pp. 48–9.

Priory stables as seen from the courtyard.

Old pump formerly at the entrance to the stables courtyard.

CHEYNEY COURT AND THE PRIOR'S GATE

Cheyney Court presents one of the most beautiful and picturesque sights in Winchester. The effect in May, when the wisteria is in bloom, is quite magical.

But its importance throughout the Middle Ages was immense, for it was here that the Bishop of Winchester held his court and administered justice. The Bishop was absolute ruler under the King of the city and a great part of its surroundings. It was in Cheyney Court that ruffians and wrongdoers were judged, and perhaps sent to sit in the Bishop's stocks near St Swithun's Bridge, or even be flung into dungeons beneath the Keep at Wolvesey Castle.

Cheyney Court and the Prior's Gate. 'Cheyney' is derived from an old oak tree which used to stand here, the French for oak being *chêne*.

THE CLOSE WALL

When you leave the Close, going through the Priory Gateway (*see* plan on pp. 48–9), it is worth glancing up at the massive Close wall, which was built to surround the monastic precincts. This was built on the foundations of a previous wall, built on the orders of St Swithun himself, who was keenly aware of the need to defend the city and its religious foundations from the marauding Danes.

Exterior view of Prior's Gate and the Close wall.

Another view of the wall, showing its enormous height.

THE LOCKBOURNE (OR LOCKBURN)

The former complex of monastic buildings naturally required a constant supply of clean water and this was cunningly arranged by diverting St Aethelwold's Stream – seen on the extreme right of the plan of the Close on pp. 48–9.

Visitors to the Deanery Garden may still see traces of the Lockbourne, but unfortunately, this is possible only on rare occasions. It is interesting, however, to trace the winding course of the Lockbourne on the map. As noted on p. 53, a solitary pump by the old Priory stables lies exactly over its course as it flows out under the south wall of the Close.

The Arms of the City of Winchester.

PART TWO

THE CITY OF WINCHESTER

The arms of the city of Winchester depict five castles and a couple of lions. In heraldic terms, the correct description runs as follows:

> Gules five Castles triple towered in saltire Argent masoned proper the Portcullis of each part-raised Or and on either side of the castle in fess point a Lion passant guardant that to the dexter contourné Gold.

This somewhat esoteric language says it all. It is a proud and ancient shield, though some people may wonder why there is no crest or motto, and why there are no supporters either side of it.

The answer is simple – Winchester's arms derive from the time when heraldry hadn't developed all those 'extras' which feature on most coats of arms. The lions are the Royal Lions, or 'Lions of England', and the castles come from a seal of the time of Edward I, who in 1276 held the very first English parliament in Winchester's Great Hall (*see* p. 64).

WILLIAM THE CONQUEROR'S CASTLE

When William the Conqueror settled in Winchester, his first priority within weeks of his victory at the Battle of Hastings was to build an impregnable castle for himself. Ruthlessly, six centuries later, Oliver Cromwell blew it up, besieging the Royalist sympathisers defending Winchester. Today, the only part left of the castle's complex of buildings is the Great Hall at the top of the High Street (see p. 64) – but this was built in the thirteenth century by Henry III, William the Conqueror's great-great-great-grandson.

We can only guess at the details, but the pictures below were drawn in the seventeenth century, when memories must still have been reasonably fresh. The whole area within its surrounding wall was rather more than 4 acres. Foundations of parts of it are still to be seen near the entrance to the Great Hall.

West view of Winchester's former castle.

East view of Winchester's former castle.

SOME FACTS ABOUT WINCHESTER CASTLE

An early dramatic episode in the history of Winchester Castle took place in 1100, when William Rufus had been killed by an arrow in the New Forest. Rufus's younger brother, Henry, galloped as fast as he could to the castle to seize the royal treasure. He forcefully persuaded the Norman nobles that he really was the rightful heir. He then made the 60-mile dash for London, and in just two days managed to get himself crowned king. His elder brother, Robert, who arguably should have inherited the throne, was conveniently out of the country. This episode was a major turning point in English history.

* * *

During the twelfth century, the Domesday Book was kept here. This was the royal inventory of what the whole country contained.

* * *

In 1135, during the civil war between the supporters of King Stephen and those of his cousin, the Empress Matilda, Winchester Castle came under siege from Henry of Blois, the Bishop of Winchester. The bishop had switched sides, and had decided to support his brother Stephen instead of his niece Matilda. The bishop set fire to the city and forced Matilda to flee from the castle.

* * *

Among the places formerly existing within the castle were a herb garden, a bird house, a treasury, several chapels and a gaol.

* * *

Henry II held his wife, Queen Eleanor (Eleanor of Aquitaine) under house arrest for plotting and supporting their sons against him. Winchester Castle was one of the places where he held her prisoner. She was only released on Henry's death – after twelve years of confinement.

* * *

French forces captured Winchester Castle in 1216, during the reign of King John, led by Louis, son of Philip II of France. The English managed to recapture the castle the following year, but only after a fortnight's battering of the defences.

* * *

In 1282, when the last native Prince of Wales, Llywelyn ap Gruffydd, was killed in a skirmish in Wales, Edward I ordered that his carcass be chopped into pieces and one quarter sent to Winchester to be fixed onto a parapet on the castle.

* * *

In 1326, Queen Isabella, wife of Edward II, had the head of Hugh Despenser, Earl of Winchester, stuck on a spike above Winchester Castle.

* * *

Queen Isabella had Edmund of Woodstock decapitated on the green below the castle walls.

* * *

In 1607 the castle passed into private hands. The last owner, Sir William Waller, sold it to the justices of the peace for Hampshire for £100.

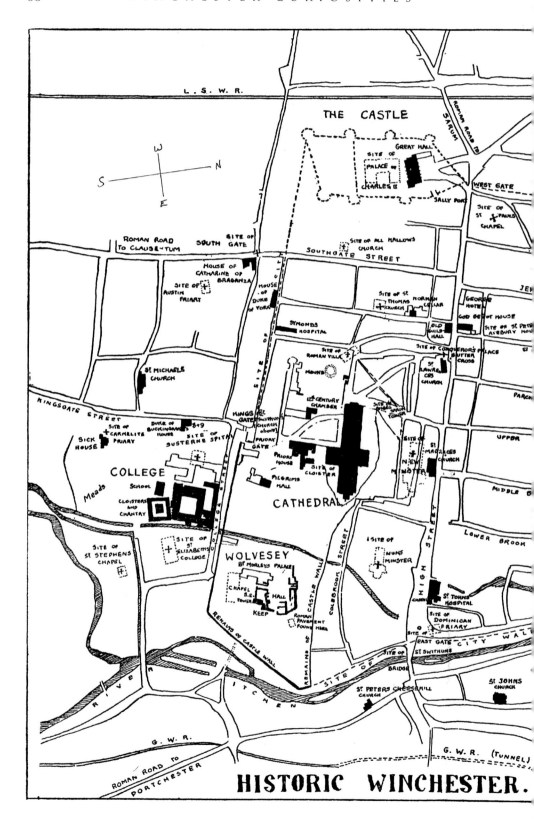

HISTORIC WINCHESTER.

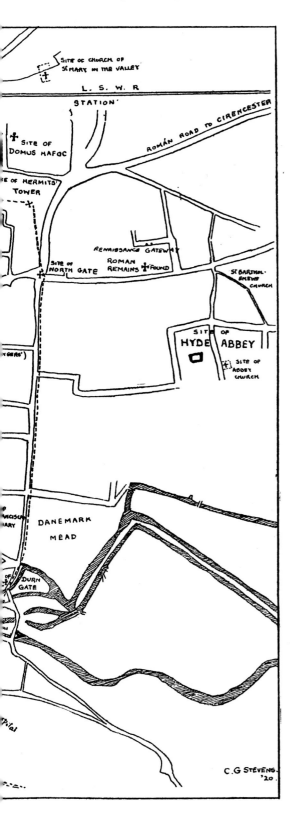

SITE OF CHURCH OF
ST MARY IN THE VALLEY

L. S. W. R

STATION

ROMAN ROAD TO CIRENCESTER

SITE OF
DOMUS MAFOC

E OF HERMITS'
TOWER

RENAISSANCE GATEWAY

SITE OF
NORTH GATE

ROMAN
REMAINS FOUND

ST BARTHOL·
EMEWS
CHURCH

SITE OF
HYDE ABBEY

SITE OF
ABBEY
CHURCH

GERS')

DANEMARK
MEAD

MCISU
ARY

DURN
GATE

C.G STEVENS.
'20.

This map was drawn by C.G. Stevens, a
pupil at Winchester College in 1920. It
is interesting to compare this with the
drawing of the city on pp. 96–7.

WINCHESTER'S ANSWER TO VERSAILLES

In 1665 Charles II brought his court to Winchester to avoid the London plague. He was so enchanted with the city that he decided to build a gigantic palace for himself on the site of the recently demolished castle (*see* p. 58). He intended it as a rival to Louis XIV's palace at Versailles.

Sir Christopher Wren produced a superb design, as shown below. A series of steps leading down from the palace would have led directly to the cathedral. Work began, and the palace was well advanced towards completion when Charles II suddenly died in 1685. Sadly, work then ceased. The unfinished palace had a chequered history, and later became a barracks – a modernised version of which still plays an important part in Winchester's long military history.

At the top of the opposite page is a sketch, as seen from the cathedral tower, of what Winchester might have looked like. It shows the whole imaginary vista of how the palace and cathedral would have been linked. At the bottom of the opposite page is a photograph taken from the cathedral roof, showing the modern Peninsular Barracks on the top of the hill, standing where the unfinished palace once stood.

Sir Christopher Wren's design for Charles II's palace at Winchester.

An artist's impression of 'The King's House', as Wren's palace was called. The roof of the west front of the cathedral is seen at the bottom of the picture.

Below: A modern photograph taken from the roof of the cathedral showing the same scene but with the military Peninsular Barracks instead of the palace.

THE GREAT HALL

Henry III, who was born in Winchester and who liked to call himself 'Henry of Winchester', ordered this Great Hall to be built in 1222 when he was just 15, and he was 28 when it was completed. Next to Westminster Hall, it is the second largest medieval hall in England: 111ft long, and 55ft wide, divided into a nave and two aisles by two rows of elegantly slender Purbeck marble columns.

Henry III held the first parliament here in 1265. It was also the scene of much royal feasting, including the banquet given by Henry VIII in 1522 for the Holy Roman Emperor, Charles V, father of Philip of Spain. And it was here in 1603 that the trial of Sir Walter Raleigh took place, at which Raleigh was found guilty of treason, taken to the Tower of London and executed thirteen years later.

In more recent times, Queen Elizabeth II and Philip, Duke of Edinburgh, had lunch here when the Queen presented Maundy Money to the cathedral in 1979.

Interior of the Great Hall, showing the Round Table hanging on the wall. (*John Crook*)

'KING ARTHUR'S ROUND TABLE'
FACT AND FABLE

One of Winchester's most famous possessions is 'King Arthur's Round Table', which hangs on the west wall of the Great Hall. It has become Winchester's top tourist icon, appearing on postcards, tea towels, chocolate wrappings and an ever-growing number of souvenirs. King Arthur, whoever he was, would have been amazed!

In 1977–8 it was subjected to the closest scientific examination, thoroughly cleaned and re-hung. Carbon dating and analysis of tree-rings in the wood both point to a probable date for its manufacture being between 1250 and 1350. More precisely, it is thought that the table was probably made for Edward I's visit to Winchester in 1290, accompanied by his family and a large company of knights, nobles and bishops.

It was a splendid occasion: political marriages were arranged, a royal tournament was enjoyed, and finally a sumptuous feast – at which the main guests would have sat around the great table, using it for the first time. The castle had been specially decorated and improved for months beforehand, and the table would have been a centrepiece at these royal celebrations.

Sir Thomas Malory tells how King Arthur received the Round Table as a wedding gift from his father-in-law:

. . . And Merlin went forth to King Leodegraunce of Camelot, and told him of the desire of King Arthur that he would have to his wife Guenever his daughter.

'That is to me,' said King Leodegraunce, 'the best tidings that ever I heard, that so worthy a king of prowess and nobleness will wed my daughter: and . . . I shall send him a gift that shall please him . . . for I shall give him the Table Round, the which Uther Pendragon gave me. . .

And so King Leodegraunce delivered his daughter, Guenever, unto Merlin, and the Table Round, with the Hundred knights . . .

When King Arthur heard of the coming of Guenever, and the hundred knights of the Round Table, he made great joy for their coming, and said, openly, 'This fair lady is passing welcome to me, for I loved her long, and therefore there is nothing so pleasing to me; and these knights with the Round Table please me more than right great riches.

Morte d'Arthur by Sir Thomas Malory, *c.* 1470

WHO WAS KING ARTHUR?

Much has been written about King Arthur, but even his most enthusiastic admirers must admit that they know very little about him.

A legendary history of Arthur was written in about 1135 by Geoffrey of Monmouth; Sir Thomas Malory wrote his prose romance *Morte d'Arthur* in the late fifteenth century; and Lord Tennyson wrote *Idylls of the King* in the middle of the nineteenth century.

If Arthur existed at all, he was a British (i.e. Celtic) leader in the west of England fighting against the invading Saxons, possibly around the year 500.

He is supposed to have fought a series of stupendous battles, beginning at 'Mount Badon' (which may have been Bath), and finishing with a defeat at 'Camlann' (perhaps Cadbury Castle in Somerset), where he was wounded.

We are left with an image of Arthur being taken away to Avalon to be healed. According to Geoffrey of Monmouth, Arthur was born at Tintagel in Cornwall and is buried at Glastonbury.

King Arthur's Round Table. (*John Crook*)

DECIPHERING THE TABLE

The words painted on the Round Table are difficult to read, but it's easier when you know what to look for.

The two words on each side of the king's head are simply KING ARTHUR, but this image of the king's face is probably that of Henry VIII himself, who had the table painted when he entertained the Holy Roman Emperor in 1522. Henry wanted to impress the Emperor with the antiquity of his ancestral claim to the throne.

Reading clockwise around the Tudor rose in the middle, are the words:

Thys is the rownde table of kyng Arthur w[ith] xxiiii of hys namyde kny*ttes

Reading clockwise around the perimeter of the table, and starting to the right of 'King Arthur' (as we look at him) are the following names of twenty-four knights. (It is important to note that each name begins with 'S' crossed by a diagonal stroke – an abbreviation for 'Sir'.)

1. galahallt	9. blubrys	17. kay
2. launcelot deulake	10. lacotemale tayle	18. Ectorde mary
3. gauen	11. lucane	19. dagonet
4. p(er)cyvale	12. plomyde	20. degore
5. lyonell	13. lamorak	21. brumear
6. trystram delyens	14. bor(s) de ganys	22. lybyus dysconyus
7. garethe	15. Safer	23. Alynore
8. bedwere	16. pelleus	24. mordrede

Some of these names are familiar to us thanks to Sir Thomas Malory and Alfred Lord Tennyson – though the spellings are somewhat different. 'Galahallt', for example, is Sir Galahad, and 'bedwere' is Sir Bedevere. But did they ever really exist? It would be pleasant to think they did. Certainly they have been granted immortality in Winchester, thanks to this extraordinary artefact.

THE WESTGATE

Sadly, Winchester's North Gate, South Gate and East Gate were all demolished in the eighteenth century. Only Kingsgate and Westgate remain. For centuries all of these gates were locked at night, keeping Winchester safe against attack and, if necessary, quarantined against the plague (*see* p. 70).

Luckily, the city authorities didn't demolish the Westgate with the others, because at that time it was an annexe to a pub – and this was far too precious to lose!

In its time the Westgate has served as a guardhouse and debtors' prison, and the worst kind of criminals were kept in squalor in a cell below the debtors, starving and forced to beg for food from passers-by.

Today it is a museum, exhibiting fascinating items linked to Winchester's past – among which visitors can enjoy seeing:

Fetters and 'gyves' for shackling prisoners' limbs
The gibbet, for exhibiting dead prisoners
Weapons, armour and ancient cannon-balls
The 'City Moot Horn' for summoning meetings
The city coffer, with its four separate locks
The standard bushel and other weights and measures of the realm
    (Winchester had the honour of keeping these official measures)

Of special interest within the museum are the graffiti carved on the wall by the wretched debtors formerly imprisoned here. And don't miss out on climbing onto the roof, from which there are splendid views of the city.

Today the view of the Westgate looking up at it from the High Street presents a picturesque exit to the town. Traffic went through it until as late as 1959. And looking at it from the other side, as you approach the city from the west, you can see the projecting 'machicolation' through which defenders of the gate could throw rocks and scalding water (or worse) down on any attackers.

The two slits with round bases were gun ports, made for hand-held cannon, and the gaping mouths of the two curious heads were the holes through which passed the chains of the drawbridge (*see* p. 115).

Above: The Westgate as it is today.

Left: The Westgate as it was in 1828.

A seventeenth-century three-masted ship, carved on a wall in the Westgate by one of the prisoners held there.

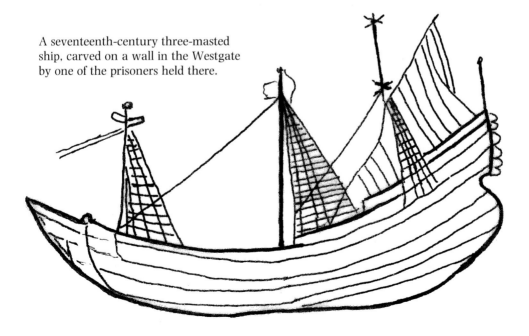

THE PLAGUE OBELISK

Just a short distance from the Westgate, further up the hill to the right, is an interesting monument commemorating the plague of 1666.

In times of plague it was possible to lock the city gates and control all comings and goings – and if it were deemed necessary, the city authorities forbade anyone to enter or leave the city.

It became the custom for country folk to bring their garden and farm produce to this point *outside* the Westgate and leave them there. They would then retire to a distance while the citizens of Winchester came out to collect the fruit and vegetables. The townsfolk would leave their money in payment in a large bowl of vinegar, in order to disinfect it – and then, when they had gone back into the city through the Westgate, the farmers and countrymen would come back and fish out the coins with pincers, thus avoiding any possible infection.

This obelisk, erected in 1759, incorporates stone slabs actually used at that time.

A HOG, A MAN AND A HORSE
WHY THE PIG?

Just a turnip-throw to the north-east of the Westgate is this splendid porker. He stands just outside the entrance to the Hampshire County Council offices. So who, or what, is he?

He is a 'Hampshire Hog' – the traditional nickname given to a native of Hampshire. The name comes from the country's famous breed of pigs.

Don't forget to look at the top of the council offices, where there is a golden hog surmounting the spire.

The Hampshire Hog.

WHO'S THE MAN ON THE HORSE?

Just an arrow-shot down the High Street from the Westgate is this impressive statue, simply entitled 'Horse and Rider' by Dame Elisabeth Frink (1930–93). Like most of her work, it has an enigmatic, timeless dignity. Standing as it does in Winchester's High Street, it can evoke thoughts of centuries of human occupation, dramatic moments of history and dominant power.

The site of 'High Street' was a pathway down to the River Itchen for thousands of years, trodden by Celts long before the Romans ever dreamed of coming here. Frink's statue seems to sum up this measureless past.

'Horse and Rider'.

QUEEN EMMA'S GIFT TO THE CITY
GOD BEGOT HOUSE

This beautiful old house has a strange history. The original 'Manor of Goudbeyete' or 'Godbiete' belonged to no less important a personage than Queen Emma, wife of Ethelred the Unready and then of King Canute.

When he married Emma, King Ethelred gave her the entire city of Winchester as a wedding present! And when she died, she willed this particular manor house to the Prior and monks of St Swithun.

But in this will she added a most extraordinary clause – for she decreed that the manor was to be 'toll free and tax free for ever'. And just to underline how above the law this property was to be, a Court Roll of the time declared: 'If any man or woman for any felony claim the liberty of Godbeat and enter it in any house or place of the same may bide and dwell safe from any officer. *And no minister of the King neither of none other Lords shall do any execution within the bounds of the said Manor, but only the minister of the said Prior and Convent of St Swithun.*'

The spelling of this has been modernised, and the italics added – but the crucial fact is that for centuries afterwards – right up until Henry VIII abolished all the monasteries – the Manor of God Begot was a safe refuge for any rogue or criminal. Much to their fury, the city authorities had no power whatsoever to intervene or even enter this sanctuary. It became the source of much friction and annoyance.

Eventually, the Manor of God Begot passed into the hands of the Dean and

Chapter, and the old privileges of sanctuary passed into oblivion. The front of what we see today is modern – though very successfully keeping an Elizabethan appearance. However, the interior and the side of the building in Royal Oak Passage, shown on the opposite page, are genuinely and robustly Elizabethan.

God Begot House in the High Street.

THE NAME 'GOD BEGOT'

The name God Begot is a puzzle. There are many versions of its spelling and equally as many explanations of its meaning have been suggested.

In fact, the manor was a very important trading centre even before it was given to Emma as a part of her wedding gift in 1002. Although the name 'Domus Godbiete' was once thought to mean 'A house granted to God', the name is now believed to have a commercial rather than a religious meaning. Today, most historians agree that 'God Begot' probably means 'a good bargain'.

Royal Oak Passage, with God Begot House on the left. The Royal Oak pub (on the right) claims to have the oldest bar in England.

THE PRIOR'S CURSE ON ANYONE TRYING
TO DEFY THE RIGHTS OF GOD BEGOT

MAY THAT MAN'S BODY DECAY, AND MAY HIS SOUL
BE DRAWN OUT OF HIM BY THE DEVIL'S HOOK;
MAY HE BE BOILED IN THE CAULDRON OF SATHANAS,
AND MAY THE BUTCHERS OF HELL
CARVE HIS FLESH FOR EVER

LONG LIVE GOOD QUEEN ANNE!

Opposite God Begot House is an ordinary high street bank. But it is a building that has enjoyed an important past, for it was once Winchester's Guildhall. Of special interest is the statue high up near the large overhanging town clock.

The figure represented is that of Queen Anne, who reigned from 1702 to 1714, and it was put here after her visit to Winchester in 1705, accompanied by her husband and consort, Prince George of Denmark. The mayor and citizens received them with rapture, for the previous three monarchs, James II and William and Mary, had ignored the city completely, and Charles II's proposed palace at the top of the hill was languishing in an unfinished state.

To everyone's joy, Queen Anne decided that she would go ahead with the palace, and present it to Prince George for his future dwelling. At last Winchester seemed to have a prosperous royal future, and might well again become the home of kings.

But alas, Queen Anne died young – and Prince George died even earlier. So this tiny statue is a kind of sad farewell to hopes that Winchester might regain its former glory. With the passing of Anne, no subsequent king or queen ever showed an interest in Charles's great scheme, designed so superbly by Christopher Wren.

The Latin inscription near the statue is: *Anna Regina Anno Pacifico 1713* – 'Queen Anne in the Year of Peace 1713', referring to the signing of the Peace of Utrecht. But in 1714, Queen Anne was dead.

THE CURFEW BELL

Above Queen Anne's statue is an elegant cupola which contains Winchester's curfew bell. It is still rung every night at 8 o'clock – and indeed so it should, for it was in Winchester in the eleventh century that William the Conqueror first ordered that the curfew should be rung every night throughout the land. It has rung in Winchester ever since.

'Curfew' is derived from the old French *couvrefeu* – 'to cover the fire' – a precaution against accidentally setting the city's timber and thatched houses alight during the night.

Statue of Queen Anne on the former City Guildhall in the High Street.

THE CITY CROSS

No one knows how or when the City Cross was first set up here. It was possibly put up about 1450, and may have been the gift of Cardinal Beaufort – but even then it might have been a replacement for an earlier one.

Like so much of Winchester, it has had its moments of vandalism, but it survived the horrors of the sixteenth century (Henry VIII), and of the seventeenth century (Oliver Cromwell). It almost disappeared in the eighteenth century when a local squire, Thomas Dummer, bought it from the Mayor and Corporation, intending it as a kind of 'gothick' folly for his estate at Cranbury Park.

When Squire Dummer's men arrived with large wagons to take it away, the citizens of Winchester gathered in high dudgeon and drove them away with strong threats of dire vengeance if they ever dared to return! Dummer's men fled. They knew when they were beaten!

The only genuinely old figure is that of St John the Evangelist, on the south side. The other larger statues depict William of Wykeham, with the book of statutes of his college, and his pastoral staff; Laurence de Anne, Mayor of Winchester; and Alfred the Great. In the top niches are Saints Thomas, Maurice, John, Peter, Laurence, Bartholomew, Swithun, and also the Blessed Virgin. These later figures were added when Gilbert Scott restored the cross in 1865.

An early nineteenth-century engraving of the City Cross. Note the girl on the right is drawing water at an old pump.

THE SITE OF WILLIAM THE CONQUEROR'S PALACE

The shops adjoining the City Cross and the area behind them towards the cathedral stand on the site of William the Conqueror's palace and chapel. About six months before the battle of Hastings, on St George's Day in 1066, a great fire destroyed the cluster of Saxon buildings built here. It was on this derelict bit of ground that the Conqueror decided to make his dwelling.

It must have been far too small to be dignified by the title of palace, but this was the Conqueror's home while the great castle at the top of today's High Street was being built.

The plaque at the entrance to St Lawrence's church – site of the Conqueror's Chapel.

Memorial plaque to Giles King Lyford.

Today, it is a baker's shop and café. It is pleasant to buy cakes there and think that King William must have eaten something similar on this very spot. The cellars throughout the area can bear testimony to this ancient past.

In the small passageway near the City Cross, leading into Great Minster Street, it is worthwhile looking at the carved Norman stonework on the right-hand wall as you pass through, which may have been part of the original Norman palace.

To the left is a sign pointing visitors into the tiny church of St Lawrence, which is the site of the chapel of the Conqueror's palace. Understandably, no trace of that chapel now remains, except perhaps in its foundations. Just inside, on the wall to the right is a memorial tablet to Giles King Lyford, the doctor who tried, in vain, to cure Jane Austen when she came to Winchester.

The history of the chapel is one of destructions and renewals. The original royal chapel was destroyed in 1143, during the civil war between King Stephen and his cousin, the Empress Matilda. It was rebuilt in 1150, and this in turn was rebuilt in 1449.

The building is still a parish church in the centre of Winchester which has a very special tradition, for each time a new bishop is to be enthroned, he first comes to St Lawrence's to pray and to put on his bishop's robes. Then he tolls one of the bells, thus 'ringing himself into his office'. Then, wearing cope and mitre, and carrying his pastoral staff, he goes out to meet the Mayor and chief citizens, and together they process into the cathedral for the enthronement service.

THE ECLIPSE INN AND A HORRIFIC EXECUTION

Beyond St Lawrence's church, round the corner on the left, is the Eclipse Inn, which was formerly the church's rectory. When it became an inn, the owner named it 'The Eclipse' as it was in direct competition with another pub close by, called 'The Sun'. Obviously the arrival of his new pub 'eclipsed' the older one!

The Square, where the City Museum now stands, was once the scene of public executions, always accompanied by the solemn tolling of St Lawrence's bell. No execution was more dramatic or terrible than that of Dame Alice Lisle, a victim of the notorious Judge Jeffreys, at the Bloody Assizes in 1685.

Alice Lisle had helped to hide two fugitives from the battle of Sedgemoor, who had taken part in the treasonable rebellion by the Duke of Monmouth. By hiding them, Dame Alice, aged 70, was considered to have committed treason herself and Judge Jeffreys insisted that the jury should declare her to be guilty. Jeffreys then ordered her to be burned alive that very afternoon!

The clergy of the cathedral led the popular outcry against such a savage punishment, and obtained a delay of five days. As a gesture of mercy, Judge Jeffreys commuted the sentence to that of being beheaded.

Dame Alice was held captive in this building, which was then still a rectory, and spent her last night here. She

The Eclipse Inn in The Square.

was taken out from here via an upper window and led to the scaffold, meeting her execution with calmness and courage. A plaque on the wall of the museum immediately opposite records this dreadful moment in Winchester's history.

Reputedly, the upper rooms and corridors of the Eclipse Inn are haunted, perhaps by Alice Lisle herself. Over the centuries many people have told of their experiences, sensing the ghost by sight, sound and smell.

GHOSTS DWELLING IN WINCHESTER

Dame Alice Lisle is certainly not the only ghost to have been seen in Winchester. The earliest recorded phantom was none other than that of King Alfred himself, frequently seen by monks as he wandered into his own recently built New Minster (see p. 107).

Here's a selection of some of the many spooky happenings which have been reported in the Close and city:

A limping monk was frequently seen moving from the garden of a house in the Close, passing right through a wall and gliding into the cathedral. When the wall was pulled down in the 1960s, three skeletons were discovered. Their bones were dated as being medieval, and one of them had obviously suffered from arthritis – probably causing him to limp. Once these skeletons were reburied, the limping monk never haunted the garden again.

Chanting in Latin has been heard in another house in the Close, and also the drumming of feet on stone paving at regular set times. People hearing these sounds have attributed them to the footfalls of monks going to their evening service in the cathedral. Strange openings and closings of doors by unseen presences have also been seen in this house.

Spectral horsemen ride through the Close and down Dome Alley. They gallop straight through the walls.

Phantom figures in medieval clothing appeared on a photograph taken in 1957. They were standing by the high altar in Winchester Cathedral. Experts could find no explanation when they examined the picture.

A smiling man in a black, high-collared coat with brass buttons haunted a house in Quarry Road. Other paranormal happenings included a musty smell, the figure of a nun, a woman in white, disembodied voices, and inexplicable movements of household objects. The house was twice exorcised, but the hauntings only became worse. . . .

A fat man in a frock coat and a three-cornered hat startled a member of a working party cleaning out the dungeons of the Great Hall of Winchester Castle in 1973. The apparition intruded into the cell and silently disappeared as he walked through a 2ft thick wall. The workman was left in a state of shock.

A First World War soldier has been seen in the wings of the Theatre Royal in Jewry Street. He has been identified as a young man who worked as a spotlight operator before being called up. He was sent to the front line and killed. The day after his mother received notice of his death, his ghost appeared in the theatre, causing an actress to faint with horror.

John Simpkins also haunts the Theatre Royal. Together with his brother James, John Simpkins built the theatre in 1913, converting a hotel which formerly stood on the site. James had the initials 'JS' included in the decorations over the stage – however, this aggrieved John, who thought the initials should have been 'J & JS'. James promised to alter the initials, but never got round to it. John never stopped being annoyed about this, even after his death! His restless spirit is seen to walk out of his former office to one of the boxes by the stage and peer intently at the decorations to see whether they have been changed.

An operatic aria has been heard, sung by a man's voice, in the basement of Winchester Library, next to the theatre in Jewry Street. The library is quite separate from any other building, however. Staff find the place 'scary' at night, and footsteps have been heard by the caretaker in the locked, empty building.

A disgruntled bedclothes snatcher used to create a nuisance in the Hyde Tavern in Hyde Street. A story tells how a former landlord turned a beggar woman away one winter's night, only to find her frozen body outside the inn the next morning. Since then, on many occasions, guides, and even the landlord and his wife used to find their bedclothes pulled off their beds. No matter how tightly the bedclothes were tucked in, the phantom bedclothes snatcher always managed to pull them off!

This carved stone is set into the side of the City Museum – opposite the Eclipse Inn – as a reminder of the execution of Dame Alice Lisle, which took place on that spot in 1685. Her ghost is said to dwell in the inn.

A TOMBSTONE RECOMMENDING SOLDIERS TO DRINK STRONG BEER

A famous tombstone in the cathedral churchyard was originally put up in 1764 in memory of Thomas Thetcher, a young soldier who died, apparently, as a result of drinking 'cold small beer' (weak beer). It is a warning to other soldiers to avoid the same fate – by drinking strong beer instead!

Thetcher's tombstone and the West Front of the cathedral.

Soldiers billeted in Winchester have valued this wise advice ever since, and have tried to maintain the tombstone in good shape. The last time it was replaced was by the Royal Hampshire Regiment in 1966. It is to be found near a yew tree to the right of the path going from the museum to the West Front of the cathedral, almost directly opposite the entrance door on the West Front. The lettering is becoming less distinct, so the wording is given here, along with a photograph to help show where it lies in relation to the West Front.

In Memory of
THOMAS THETCHER
Grenadier in the north Reg.
Of Hants Militia, who died of a
Violent Fever contracted by drinking
Small Beer when hot the 12th of May
1764. Aged 26 Years.

In grateful remembrance of whose universal
Good will towards his Comrades, this Stone
Is placed here at their expence, as a small
Testimony of their regard and concern.

Here sleeps in peace a Hampshire Grenadier,
Who caught his death by drinking cold small Beer.
Soldiers, be wise from his untimely fall
And when ye're hot drink Strong or none at all

This memorial being decay'd was restored
By the Officers of the Garrison, A.D. 1781

An honest Soldier never is forgot
Whether he die by Musket or by Pot.

OLDER NAMES OF WINCHESTER

As a town, Winchester is older than recorded history, and has been given a number of names by its various occupants. In chronological order, Winchester has been known as:

Ouenta: The name given by Ptolemy (*c.* AD 90–168), the Egyptian astronomer and geographer. This name appears in his work *Geographia*, written about AD 150.

Caer Gwent: The name used by the ancient Britons before the Romans came. The word 'Caer' is also found in a number of Welsh place names such as Caernarfon, and means 'fort'. The word 'Gwent' is also found in Welsh place names, meaning 'place'.

Venta Belgarum: The name of Winchester used by the Romans. It means 'market-place of the Belgae', and 'venta' still survives, somewhat disguised, in the first part of the name, 'Winchester'.

Uintancaestir: The name used by the Venerable Bede in about AD 730. 'Ceastir' (and its various forms) means 'fort' or 'camp'.

Wintonia: The name used by Asser, in about AD 894, in his biography of Alfred the Great.

ANTHONY TROLLOPE'S 'BARCHESTER'

Let us suppose that Barchester is a quiet town in the west of England, more remarkable for the beauty of its cathedral and the antiquity of its monuments than for any commercial prosperity; that the west end of Barchester is the cathedral close, and that the aristocracy of Barchester are the bishop, dean and canons, with their respective wives and daughters. . . .

The Warden, 1855

THOMAS HARDY'S 'WINTONCESTER'

. . . WINTONCESTER, that fine old city, aforetime capital of Wessex . . . the broad cathedral tower, with its Norman windows and immense length of aisle and nave ... the tower of the College . . . the ancient hospice, where to this day the pilgrim may receive his dole of bread and ale. . . .

Tess of the D'Urbervilles, 1891

HISTORIC STREET NAMES

Unfortunately, some of Winchester's medieval street names were changed in the nineteenth century, losing something of their links with the past. 'High Street' was once *Cheapside*; 'Upper Brook Street' was *Sildworten Street*, where the silver workers worked; 'St Peter's Street' was *Flescmangers Street*, where the 'flesh-mongers' or butchers had their shops. (The full name of the church which once stood here was St Peter's-in-the-Shambles, which brings to mind York's famous 'Shambles', meaning butchers' market stalls.)

Nevertheless, there are still names which ring with history. One of the most important of these is Jewry Street, running from High Street to the former Northgate. This area was the site of a large Jewish community who lived and traded here  during the Middle Ages. Jews came to England in Norman times, but were banned from the country in 1290, not returning to England until the seventeenth century, in the time of Oliver Cromwell. The original significance of the name 'Jewry Street' has therefore been out of date for over 700 years!

PARCHMENT STREET has retained its name since the Middle Ages, literally being the place where parchment was made. Parchment-making was an important industry, particularly in a city of scholars and churchmen. Books and documents were handwritten on these specially-treated animal skins, the finest of which were called 'vellum'. It wasn't until the fifteenth century that paper began to replace parchment.

TANNERS' STREET has kept the name linking it with that particular trade, but SOUTHGATE STREET, although sounding authentic, as it reminds us that there used to be a 'Southgate' standing there, was formerly called Gold Street, where jewellers plied their trade.

CHESIL STREET, where the Old Chesil Rectory stands, is named after the flinty pebbles of the riverside (*see* p. 86).

All goods coming from the east and brought up from the River Itchen would come through the Eastgate, which is now remembered only in the name Eastgate Street. And there was a smaller gate which let into the self-explanatory North Walls, now remembered only in the name of Durngate and Durngate Place.

The name of STAPLE GARDENS is a reference to the time when Winchester had the privilege of being one of the Staple towns in the country. This meant that its wool merchants had a monopoly of purchase and export. This area of Staple Gardens was where these merchants had their warehouses and the 'King's beam', which held the standard scales and weights for weighing wool.

THE PENTICE is one of the distinctive parts of the High Street, with its wooden columns supporting an open corridor along a row of shops. The name is a variation on 'penthouse' and is linked linguistically with the word 'appendage'. 'Pentice' is derived from the French *appentis*, meaning 'shed' or 'lean-to'.

Old shop-keepers' trade signs hanging opposite the Pentice: a boot and a teapot.

'THE BROOKS' – OLD AND NEW

It is almost impossible to imagine Winchester as it once was, even a couple of centuries ago. Nowadays, the modern area called the Brooks Shopping Centre is a thriving scene, bustling with twenty-first century life. However, the name of 'The Brooks' was a reality in bygone times, when this low-lying part of Winchester contained streams running through them. The pictures below show just how different twenty-first century lifestyle has become.

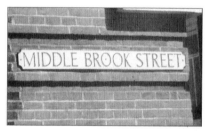

Above: The sign for Middle Brook Street.

Left: Middle Brook Street, in the days when a stream ran through it.

Two views of the Brooks Shopping Centre.

ABBEY HOUSE – SITE OF 'NUNNAMINSTER'

Abbey House, a beautiful eighteenth-century house situated in The Broadway, is the official residence of the Mayor of Winchester during his or her term of office. Only five cities in Britain have the distinction of possessing such an official residence for their mayors.

Abbey House was built on the site of one of Winchester's great monastic establishments founded in about AD 900 by King Alfred's widow, Queen Ealshswith, and which was known as 'Nunnaminster; or 'the nuns' abbey'. Later, it became known as 'St Mary's Abbey' and was home to an abbess and twenty-six nuns. In all, there were over a hundred people living in this religious community – officials, servants, and a number of children for whom it was a highly regarded boarding school. Like all other monasteries, it was forced to close in the 1530s by Henry VIII, and most of its buildings were demolished.

Abbey House.

Abbey House and its gardens remained in private ownership until 1889, when the City Council decided to buy it and make its grounds available for the public. Today, the gardens are a beautiful and peaceful area for all to enjoy.

The interior of Abbey House, restored to its original splendour, is now the venue for many civic functions, and is used for entertaining official guests to the city. It is not open to the public, but passers-by can enjoy the splendid coats of arms, one on each of the iron gates leading out to The Broadway (*see* p. 56).

MORE THAN 800 MAYORS

Mayors are elected annually in May by fellow members of the City Council. The office of the Mayor of Winchester is the second oldest mayoralty in England, dating back to the 1190s. The exact date is not known but it is thought that Cllr Joan Lang, Mayor in the year 2000, was possibly the 800th holder of the office.

THE OLD CHESIL RECTORY

The Old Chesil Rectory is one of the oldest houses in Winchester – dating from around 1450. It is situated just beyond the town bridge at the bottom of the High Street, on the corner of Chesil Street. It is a beautiful half-timbered building, carefully restored and rescued from threat of destruction at the end of the nineteenth century, when it was condemned as being unfit for human habitation. Today it is owned by the city authorities, and is a thriving and highly popular restaurant.

The word 'chesil' means gravel, or pebbles, and is perhaps best known in the name of 'Chesil Beach' – the extraordinary 8-mile-long ridge of shingle running from Portland to Abbotsbury in Dorset.

The name here in Winchester reminds us that during the Middle Ages, the River Itchen was wider and deeper, and navigable from Southampton. This area was then a shingle beach where ships could be anchored and goods brought into the city through the now demolished Eastgate.

THE OLD BLUE BOAR INN – THE OLDEST HOUSE IN WINCHESTER

The old Blue Boar Inn is in fact older than the Old Chesil Rectory, having been built around 1340, and is the oldest surviving home in Winchester. It is situated on what is now called Blue Ball Hill – which is probably a misnomer for 'Blue Boar'.

Two views of the Old Blue Boar Inn, built in about 1340.

In the Middle Ages there were many Blue Boar Inns and White Boar Inns throughout the country. One of the badges of Richard, Duke of York, father of Edward IV and Richard III, was 'a blewe Bore with his tuskis and his cleis (claws) and his membres of gold'. The White Boar, however, was a popular sign of Richard III.

Interestingly, when Richard III was killed at the battle of Bosworth in 1485, White Boar inn signs were painted blue, this being the easiest and cheapest way of changing the sign.

THE OLDEST OBJECTS IN WINCHESTER

What are the oldest things in Winchester? No, not the cathedral, nor the Saxon remains of the old abbeys; not even the Roman objects and mosaics on display in the museum.

The oldest things here are the numerous Sarsen Stones, sometimes called 'Druid Stones', which are scattered around the city and the surrounding area – yet most people pass them by without taking the slightest notice of them.

The word sarsen is thought to derive from the name 'Saracen' and this perhaps indicates the sense of awe and mystery which has traditionally been linked with them. No fewer than ninety stones used to be in Baring Road, on the route leading up to Giles Hill, where the famous annual fair took place in the Middle Ages. Did they have special significance? We may never know.

Sarsen Stone in the car park area of the River Park Leisure Centre.

'Druid Stones' can be found in the car park of River Park Leisure Centre; at the corner of Beggar's Lane and Blue Ball Hill; at St John's church in St John's Street; in Castle Grounds in Castle Avenue; at the 'Plague Stone' in upper High Street; in St George's Street; in Abbey Gardens (a group of three); just outside the Close Gate (Prior's Gate); at the corner of Minster Lane and St Thomas Street; at the corner of St Cross Road and Canon Street; outside Garth House in Edward Road; and at the gate of St Bartholomew's church, King Alfred Place.

Sarsen Stone at the corner of Minster Lane and St Thomas Street.

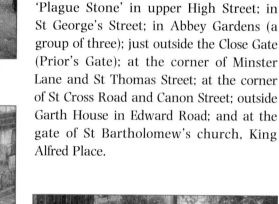

Three Sarsen Stones in Abbey Gardens.

Sarsen Stone just outside the Prior's Gate which leads into the Close.

ST SWITHUN-UPON-KINGSGATE

During the fourteenth century, according to one authority, there were no fewer than seventy-one churches in Winchester – an extraordinary number when one considers that these were in addition to the cathedral and the large abbeys. It says something for the centrally important part played by religion in those days.

Most of these churches have long disappeared – but a curious survival is St Swithun-upon-Kingsgate, a small gate to the south of the Close, within a few yards of the Close Gate (sometimes called Prior's Gate, *see* p. 55).

The entrance is not immediately obvious but is found to the right of Kingsgate as one walks away from the Close. An open door leads from the pavement and upstairs to the church above. First recorded in 1263, the church was once used by the servants of the monastery.

Coming out of the Close through Prior's Gate. The entrance to St Swithun-upon-Kingsgate can be seen just a few steps beyond Kingsgate.

A view of Kingsgate from the end of College Street. St Swithun-upon-Kingsgate is above the arch.

JANE AUSTEN'S LAST LODGING

In College Street, a short distance from Kingsgate, is the plain, elegantly simple house where Jane Austen lodged for the last six weeks of her short life. A plaque on the front wall tells us the facts, but the house is now a private dwelling owned by Winchester College, and no visitors are allowed.

Jane came here in May 1817, aged 41, obviously suffering from some illness which was never named, but which may have been Addison's disease. She had hoped to be able to go out into the city in a wheelchair, but her weakness prevented this, though she did manage one little trip out of the house in a sedan chair.

Her brother Henry, who knew the bishop because of his recent examination for ordination, may have been instrumental in gaining permission for Jane to be buried in the cathedral. According to the custom of the times, only male relations attended the service, so the only people present at her interment were her three brothers and one nephew. Her coffin was wheeled along College Street, through Kingsgate into the Close, and thence to the cathedral. Her beloved sister Cassandra remained behind.

The house in College Street
where Jane Austen died.

VENTA

When Winchester races first took their beginning
It is said the good people forgot their old Saint
Not applying at all for the leave of St Swithin
And that William of Wykeham's approval was faint.

The races however were fix'd and determin'd
The company met & weather was charming
The Lords & Ladies were sattin'd and ermin'd
And nobody saw any future alarming.

But when the old Saint was inform'd of these doings
He made but one spring from his shrine to the roof
Of the Palace which now lies so sadly in ruins
And thus he address'd them all standing aloof.

Oh, subjects rebellious, Oh Venta depraved
When once we are buried you think we are dead
But behold me Immortal. – By vice you're enslaved
You have sinn'd and must suffer. – Then further he said

These races & revels & dissolute measures
With which you're debasing a neighbouring Plain
Let them stand – you shall meet with your curse in your pleasures
Set off for your course, I'll pursue with my rain.

Ye cannot but know my command in July
Henceforward I'll triumph in shewing my powers,
Shift your race as you will it shall never be dry
The curse upon Venta in July is showers.

Jane Austen (her last piece of writing)

'Venta' (an earlier name for Winchester) was composed by Jane Austen in the last days of her life, and dictated to her sister Cassandra. A poignant moment came in the fourth verse, at the word 'dead' – which Cassandra wrote as 'gone'. Perhaps Jane could not bring herself to say 'dead', or perhaps Cassandra could not bring herself to write it. The poem was dictated on St Swithun's day (15 July) 1817, and Jane died on the 18th.

WINCHESTER COLLEGE
WILLIAM OF WYKEHAM'S GREAT SCHOOL

William of Wykeham founded The College of St Mary, Winchester, in 1382, choosing the site to be conveniently near the entrance of his Palace of Wolvesey. He had already founded New College, Oxford, in 1379, so this school, dedicated to the Virgin Mary, was planned to provide New College with a steady supply of pupils well grounded in Latin. Scholars first entered Winchester College on 28 March 1394, and, remarkably, most of the original buildings are still standing.

The main entrance, Outer Gate, still possesses its original statue of the Virgin, crowned, and with the Christ child in her arms. It is almost miraculous that such a statue should have survived the destructions of both Henry VIII and Oliver Cromwell. It is an exquisite piece of work, but often overlooked by tourists eager to go through into the ancient courtyard beyond.

In more than 700 years, Winchester College has accumulated so many customs and traditions that it would take a lifetime to discover them all. A guided tour is a must for anyone who wants to soak up its atmosphere. The main buildings have hardly changed since they were built in the fourteenth century. Before you enter Outer Gate, glance up at the roof to the right of the tower. On the ridge there is a slightly raised section. This is to allow steam to escape, for this was the brewery where the boys' beer was made. The College still possesses old jugs and wooden food platters used by scholars in bygone centuries: these are on view to visitors.

The entrance to Winchester College from College Street, showing the Virgin and Child (above the arch) and the brewery roof.

Old leather 'jacks', mug, wooden trencher, salt cellar and candlesticks used by pupils of Winchester College in bygone centuries.

'THE TRUSTY SERVANT'

A wonderfully eccentric painting hangs near the stairway leading from the College's Chamber Court. It shows an eighteenth-century servant with a pig's head, ass's ears, stag's feet, and carrying an assortment of household tools. Its symbolic purpose is to depict the most desirable qualities to be found in an ideal serving man. The virtues are explained in Latin and English verses. Put briefly, these are:

A pig's snout – to show that he isn't fussy about what he eats
A padlocked mouth – to show that he'll keep secrets
Donkey's ears – to show how patient he is
Deer's feet – to show how quickly he can run to do his errands
A hand carrying household tools – to show how industrious he is
Neatly dressed – to show that he isn't slovenly
An open hand – to show his open, trustworthy nature
Armed with sword and shield – to show that he's ready to protect his master

An earlier version of 'The Trusty Servant' was painted about 1560, wearing Elizabethan dress. It was repainted with eighteenth-century costume when George III visited the College in 1778. The College Coat of Arms is seen in the top left corner, with its famous motto:

MANNERS MAKYTH MAN

The Trusty Servant.

THE LEGEND OF THE WINCHESTER SCHOOLBOY AND THE 'MIZMAZE' ON ST CATHERINE'S HILL

St Catherine's Hill lies about a mile south-east of Winchester. It is a large round hill rising above the water meadows of the Itchen. It takes some energy and determination to climb it, but those who do so are rewarded by some fine views and the discovery, at the summit, of a curious, square, medieval 'mizmaze', measuring 90ft by 86ft. A chapel dedicated to St Catherine once stood nearby, but there is no trace of this now.

According to legend, the maze was cut into the turf by a Winchester College schoolboy, forced to stay at school during the summer holidays. The legend also has it that the same schoolboy, pining for home, wrote the school song, 'Dulce Domum' (sweet home) while up here on 'Hills' – as St Catherine's is known to Wykehamists.

Plan of the mizmaze on St Catherine's Hill.

The date of the mizmaze on St Catherine's Hill is unknown, but it is probably medieval in origin. The schoolboy legend is almost certainly mere fiction.

The hill has been a recreation area for centuries of schoolboys, and the maze itself was used (and possibly still is) for initiation rites for newcomers to the school. In 'Winchester College Notions' (1901), a collection of esoteric customs and college word lore, the writers describe 'certain ceremonies' which are required:

. . . There are certain ceremonies on and about Hills which new men have to go through on the first or second Sunday after their arrival. The new man starts immediately after dinner for Hills, and his first direction probably is to take a stone out of Chalk Pit. This he has to hold on to, whatever happens. He then delivers his top hat to his Socius, and is ready to obey the petty tyrant of the hour. For this latter is always a Junior who has been told off to look after him and teach him his Notions. To initiate the new man into these mysteries is part of his duty.

The ceremonies are as follows:
1. TO CLIMB UP CHALK PIT
2. TO TOLL ROUND LABYRINTH FROM BEGINNING TO END
3. TO KNEEL DOWN AND KISS DOMUM CROSS, DEPOSITING THE STONE HE HAD TAKEN FROM CHALK PIT, OR ELSEWHERE
4. TO TOLL ROUND TRENCH
5. TO WALK BLINDFOLD THROUGH CLUMP

'NOTIONS'

The lore of schoolboys can become incredibly arcane and complicated – and nowhere more so than at Winchester College. Over the centuries, the College's secret language and strange customs came to be known as 'Notions' – which had to be taught to all College newcomers. In 1901 a group of 'Three Beetleites' produced a book containing hundreds of 'Winchester College Notions'. Notoriously, slang words and secret languages quickly go out of date, to be replaced by others, equally short-lived – but some words stay the course for decades, if not centuries. Here are a few items taken from that collection of 1901:

ADAM AND EVE: A stream flowing from Birley's Corner through Dalmatia, running parallel to Old Barge till it rejoins New Barge immediately below First Pot.

APPLE-PIE DAY: The Thursday after the first Tuesday in Sealing Week, when College men got apple pies. On this day, which is always a Hatch Thoke, College Six play Commoner Six.

DOMUM: The Winchester Song, supposed to have been carved on Domum Tree by a man kept back for the holidays, who then committed suicide.

DOMUM CROSS: A cross in Trench on the further side of Hills. Every new man has to put into it a stone taken from Chalk Pit, and then bend down on his knees and kiss the cross.

DOMUM TREE: The elm tree on which Domum is traditionally supposed to have been carved. Domum used to be sung at evening Hills around this tree.

FOUNDER'S KIN: Those men who could trace their descent from William of Wykeham's family. They lived at the expense of the College, to which they were admitted without any further qualification . . . Thickness of skull was supposed to be a qualification of these gentlemen, and a trencher was brought into forcible contact with their heads to test their claims. If the trencher broke first, their claims were considered genuine.

HATCH THOKE: Two whole remedies or holidays kept in honour of the Founder in Cloister Time and Short Half.

NIPPERKIN: A stone jug of beer, served out in College between meals. It was stopped in 1848 when the use of tea became prevalent.

SHEEPWASH: To drag a man out of bed to the tub-room, and throw him into a tub with his nightclothes on.

TOTHERISH: Applied to anything which would be done at a tother [any other school] and not at Winchester, and so, babyish or silly. 'That is a totherish thing to do' is the most contemptuous phrase known to Wykehamists.

The CITY from St GILES HILL about 1450 AD.

Urbs Winton Circa AD MCCCCL

KEY TO S

a. College . shewing Wykeham's original Tower...........1. Kings Gate . with
b. St Stephen's Chapel ....m. Close Gate ......
c. Wolvesey Palace . SE Tower showing ledges at foot. o. City Wall
d.........ditto   Chapel . on site of present Chapel........p Close Wall } s's.
e . Great Keep - shewing columns laid in wall...........q South Gate
f. Great Hall.......g. Gateway towards Town ....r. Prior's Hovse.
h. St Michael's Church....j. Susterne Spital.........S Monk's Refect
k. Pilgrims' Hall of Monastery.................t. Cloisters.   C

RAM ...

hurch v. Cathedral. without Hunton's Lady Chapel. 9. Guild Hall..........
re it. w. Small Tower (originally Anglo Saxon)...10. Godbiete House..........
........near S:Swithun's Tomb. ——..............11. S: Peter in the Shambles.
........x. S: Thomas' Church.....................................
........y. Ruins of New Minster. z Nuns Minster 12. Castle shewing Gate
oad.. 2. S: Peter Colebroke ....13. West Gate...14 Domus Hafoc.....
nery. 3. East Gate . 4. S: John's Hostel ...15. North Gate. 16. Dung-Gate
.....5. S: Maurise 6. S: Lawrence and Remains of Conqeror's Palace...
(under t)..7. City Cross....8...Prison ...17. S: Johns...18. Hyde Abbey

WOLVESEY PALACE / CASTLE

Even in its present dilapidated state, Wolvesey Palace is an impressive sight. For many centuries it was one of the greatest buildings in England: home of the Bishops of Winchester, some of whom were second in importance only to the king at the time.

In 1302, the royal castle by the Westgate was so seriously damaged by fire that it was never occupied by royalty again. Therefore, for the next three and a half centuries, Wolvesey Palace was the lodging-place for all visiting kings, queens and important guests of Winchester's bishops.

William of Wykeham welcomed Richard II here at Wolvesey in 1393, when a parliament was held in Winchester. Ten years later, in 1403, Wykeham fêted Henry IV when he came to Winchester to marry Joanna of Navarre in the cathedral. Cardinal Beaufort hosted Henry V here before the battle of Agincourt. Henry VI came here several times to stay with Cardinal Beaufort, who was his great-uncle. And Henry VI also came to stay with Beaufort's successor, Bishop Waynflete, especially to discuss his plans to found his new school at Eton, which he was keen to model on Winchester College. And probably the greatest royal occasion of all at Wolvesey was in 1554, when Queen Mary Tudor first met Philip II here, just before their marriage in the cathedral.

It was on 28 March 1394 that the first Warden, John Morys, and the first seventy scholars of the 'Newe College of St Marie' assembled in the presence chamber of Wolvesey Palace, to be greeted and blessed by William of Wykeham himself. They then set out in solemn procession to cross the road (such as it was in those days) and enter their newly built college; a significant moment in the history of English education.

A detail from the picture on pp. 96–7. It gives some idea of what Wolvesey Palace looked like in its heyday – and it's worth noting that it lies almost directly opposite Winchester College. Wykehamists were lucky boys to have lived just across the road from where some of the pivotal moments in English history were taking place.

A BRIEF HISTORY OF WOLVESEY

In the distant past an island existed here, owned by someone with a name like 'Wulf'. It was in fact Wulf's Island – the name which later turned into Wolvesey.

Tenth century St Aethelwold built his Saxon Bishop's Palace on this site.

c. 1110   William Gifford, the second Norman Bishop of Winchester, started to build a new palace, replacing the earlier Saxon building.

c. 1130–71   Henry of Blois, the third Norman Bishop, added extensively to Gifford's palace, creating a huge bishop's residence. Over the next four and a half centuries, many succeeding bishops, in particular William of Wykeham, added more and more to the palace.

c. 1680   Bishop Morley decided to pull the palace down and replace it with a new residence in the Baroque style. The old chapel, however, was retained and can still be seen from College Street.

1786   Bishop Brownlow North demolished all except the west wing of Bishop Morley's palace. This wing is the present bishop's palace, running at right angles to College Street.

Ruins of Wolvesey Palace.

The college seen from Wolvesey Palace.

Bishop Morley's palace, with the old chapel in the background.

Bishop Morley's palace seen from the west.

JOHN KEATS COMPLETES HIS 'MARVELLOUS YEAR'

The destruction of Wolvesey Palace by Bishop Brownlow North was virtually complete in the autumn of 1819, when the rising young poet, John Keats, came to spend about a month's holiday in Winchester, staying with his friend Charles Armitage Brown. He may have lodged near the High Street, but this is uncertain. He had hoped to find a useful library in the city, but was disappointed not to find one.

1819 had been his 'Great Year' in which he had written, among other poems: 'Fancy'; 'Bards of Passion'; 'The Eve of St Agnes'; 'The Eve of St Mark'; 'Bright Star'; 'La Belle Dame sans Merci'; 'Ode to Psyche'; 'Ode to a Grecian Urn'; 'Ode to Melancholy'; 'Indolence'; 'Ode to the Nightingale' and he was working on 'Lamia', which he finished while staying in Winchester. He was also busy with 'Otho the Great' and 'The Fall of Hyperion'.

Rarely if ever has a poet produced so many poems of such quality in so short a time. Furthermore, during the summer of this year he had become unofficially engaged to his sweetheart, Fanny Brawne. Shatteringly, however, he had also experienced the first signs of tuberculosis. As a medical student, he knew his symptoms were serious, but he little realised during this relaxing time in Winchester that he had only eighteen months to live.

It was during this visit to Winchester that Keats wrote what was to prove his last major poem and his final ode, 'To Autumn', which he wrote after strolling along the river path from behind Winchester College to the Hospital of St Cross (*see* pp. 102–4).

Here is part of a letter Keats wrote to his friend and fellow poet, John Hamilton Reynolds, just a few days after writing 'To Autumn':

> . . . How beautiful the season is now. How fine the air – a temperate sharpness about it. Really, without joking, chaste weather – Dian skies. I never liked stubble-fields so much as now – aye, better than the chilly green of the Spring. Somehow, a stubble field looks warm, in the same way that some pictures look warm. This struck me so much in my Sunday's walk that I composed upon it . .
> .
>
> Winchester, 22 September 1819

The water meadows where Keats composed his poem are reached by following College Street, going beyond the college and the ruins of Wolvesey Palace, and then turning right at the end, taking the footpath to St Cross.

TO AUTUMN (*first verse*)

Season of mists and mellow fruitfulness!
   Close bosom-friend of the maturing sun;
Conspiring with him how to load and bless
   With fruit the vines that round the thatch-eaves run;
To bend with apples the moss'd cottage-trees,
   And fill all fruit with ripeness to the core;
     To swell the gourd, and plump the hazel shells
   With a sweet kernel; to set budding more,
And still more, later flowers for the bees,
Until they think warm days will never cease,
     For Summer has o'erbrimmed their clammy cells.

John Keats
Written in Winchester, 18 September 1819

John Keats (1795–1821).

ST CROSS – THE OLDEST ALMSHOUSE IN ENGLAND

The Hospital of St Cross lies about three-quarters of a mile to the south of Winchester. The quickest way to get there is by taking Southgate Street and continuing as its name changes to St Cross Road. St Cross is found down a very short lane to the left, by a little pub called The Lamb. Be warned that the lane is a dead end, and there is very little parking space.

An alternative, more leisurely way to walk to St Cross is to go past Jane Austen's house, Winchester College and Wolvesey Palace. Turn right at the end of College Street, and take the footpath leading through the water meadows where Keats found the inspiration to write his ode 'To Autumn'.

To visit St Cross is to step back in time. The hackneyed old phrase about a place where 'time stands still' is fully justified as you contemplate the lovely courtyard bounded on one side by a row of almshouses with picturesquely tall chimneys; on another by a dining hall where old men have eaten since the twelfth century; and where at one corner stands a chapel built by William the Conqueror's grandson.

The crucial thing to know about St Cross is that there are two foundations, two founders, two sets of brothers, two logos, and to distinguish one from the other, the brothers wear robes which are either black or dark red (or, properly speaking, this colour is called 'murry').

THE FIRST FOUNDER: HENRY OF BLOIS

Henry of Blois (1101–71) was one of the most important bishops Winchester has ever had, holding office for forty-two years. He was the son of William the Conqueror's daughter Adela. Immensely rich and powerful, he played a vital role in the civil war between King Stephen, his half-brother, and the Empress Matilda, his cousin. During this war, he virtually destroyed the city of Winchester by setting fire to it, hoping to drive Matilda out. However, his lasting legacy to Winchester is the Hospital of St Cross, which he founded in 1136.

The Charter of Foundation runs as follows:

Thirteen poor men, feeble and so reduced in strength that they can scarcely, or not at all, support themselves without other aid, shall remain in the same Hospital constantly; to whom necessary clothing, provided by the Prior of the establishment, shall be given, and beds fit for their infirmities; and daily a good loaf of wheaten bread of the weight of five measures, three dishes at dinner, and one for supper, and drink in sufficient quantity . . .

And beside these thirteen poor men, 100 other poor persons, as deserving as can be found and more indigent, shall be received at the hour of dinner . . .

THE SECOND FOUNDER:
CARDINAL HENRY BEAUFORT

Cardinal Henry Beaufort (1377–1447) was another immensely rich and powerful bishop of Winchester (*see* p. 19), and like Henry of Blois, held office for forty-two years. He was the half-brother of Henry IV and uncle of Henry V, and he was probably the wealthiest man in England. In 1446, a year before his death, he put forward a plan to provide another almshouse for those who once had 'everything handsome about them', but who now 'had suffered losses'. It became known as 'The Almshouse of Noble Poverty'. Today, these Brothers wear claret-coloured robes with the symbol of a cardinal's hat to distinguish them from the Brothers of the earlier foundation, who wear black robes with the symbol of the 'crutch cross'.

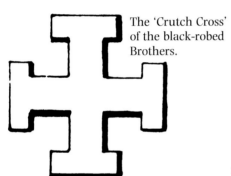

The 'Crutch Cross' of the black-robed Brothers.

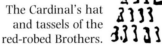

The Cardinal's hat and tassels of the red-robed Brothers.

St Cross – the Beaufort Tower, where 'The Wayfarer's Dole' is still provided.

THE CHURCH OF THE HOSPITAL OF ST CROSS

Visitors may look round this lovely church by themselves, but it's far better to be shown round by one of the Brothers. Don't miss the following curious features:

CARVINGS ON THE FIRST PILLAR as you enter the church: forbidden fruit (symbolising the Fall); water plant (Baptism); lily (Sanctification); victor's palm (Paradise).

BIRD-BEAK WINDOW in the north transept – unique in England.

SQUARE PANEL in north transept, with the hospital's motto; 'Have Mynde'.

LECTERN made of oak, with parrot's head and showing a heart. This signifies that the reader should 'read from the heart and not recite like a parrot.'

GRAFFITI on the north side of the choir, showing a coach and horses.

NORMAN FONT brought from the now demolished local church of St Faith's.

ODDLY-ANGLED WINDOW nearest the crossing on the eastern side of the north transept. Sunlight through this window falls on a pillar in the north aisle only on 3 May and 14 September, lighting up the place where a statue of the Virgin Mary once stood. The date 3 May is the date of 'The Invention of the Cross' – i.e. the date when St Helena 'found' (Latin: *invenire*) the True Cross. Of course, this was a particularly important date for the Hospital of St Cross.

The Church
of St Cross.

THE 'WAYFARER'S DOLE'

Probably the most well-known feature about St Cross is the traditional gift of the 'Wayfarer's Dole' to any visitor who asks for it.

Nowadays, the dole consists of a small piece of bread and a drink of beer, given in a special St Cross tumbler (until quite recently it was given in an old cup made from the horn of a cow). This token gesture is the continuation of a tradition going back more than 800 years. It is astonishing to remember that when Henry de Blois originally founded this almshouse, he ordered that 'apart from these thirteen poor men, 100 other poor persons . . . shall be received at the hour of dinner.'

It was a gigantic display of generosity from this hugely wealthy bishop. In days of desperate poverty and starvation, a steady supply of bread and wine would have enabled many families to survive – and it was quite in order for the poor local 'wayfarer' to come and collect food for his hungry wife and children.

'The Wayfarer's Dole' as it is given today. The 'Crutch Cross' is marked on the wooden platter. The special beer mug is also marked with a Crutch Cross. The beer is given with a piece of bread to anyone who asks for it.

THE TOWN BRIDGE AND THE CITY MILL

Returning from St Cross to the city through the water meadows, and having reached College Street again, if you continue with the riverbank on your right, you will pass a section of the city wall on your left. It is worth noting that different groups or guilds built different parts of this. There are clearly defined sections, shown by the different building materials used by the various groups. A little further along this path is a small section of the older Roman wall exposed to view.

Approaching the bottom of the city now, you will see the town bridge over the Itchen – this is the 'new' one built in 1813 replacing the first bridge, which according to tradition, was built by St Swithun in the ninth century. The plaque below is on the wall near the bridge.

Crossing the road, you come to the City Mill, now a National Trust property, which gives special displays of milling on specified days. It is well worth a visit, with a 'secret garden' at the rear.

Left: The town bridge seen from a window of the city mill.

Winchester is well served by watercourses which provided the power for 12 mills in the medieval period. The City Mill was in existence by the late 10th century when King Eadred (946-955) granted his nobleman Aethelgeard a mill at Eastgate.

By 1086 the mill was held by the priory of Wherwell, near Andover. Following the Dissolution it passed by Royal Charter to the City.

The present building dates from 1743.

HYDE ABBEY AND THE QUEST FOR ALFRED'S BONES

Alongside the Saxon cathedral, known as Old Minster, Alfred the Great founded another important monastery known as New Minster. The two buildings jostled uncomfortably close together so that the services held in one could be heard by those worshipping in the other.

The area was so crowded that in 1110, Henry I – son of the Conqueror – ordered New Minster to be demolished and its monks to resettle themselves in a newly built abbey in the north-west corner of the city. Hence Hyde Abbey was created: it was the 'new New Minster'.

Alfred the Great was originally buried in Old Minster, but a story is told that his ghost was so frequently seen wandering from his tomb there to visit his own monastery of New Minster, that the monks begged for his remains to be transferred there. This was done – and Alfred's ghost ceased its wanderings!

Naturally enough, all the precious relics belonging to New Minster were solemnly taken to Hyde Abbey: these included Alfred's bones; the remains of his wife Queen Ealswith and their son King Edward the Elder; the relics of two Saxon saints, Grimbald and Judoc; the supposed head of St Valentine; and a precious golden cross given by King Canute.

Almost unbelievably, King Alfred's tomb was completely lost when Henry VIII ordered Hyde Abbey to be destroyed. In 1788, when a prison was being built on the site, a large stone coffin encased in lead was found, containing human bones which were reburied. Then in 1866, a keen amateur archaeologist, John Mellow, dug around the site and uncovered them – if indeed they were the same bones. At any rate, he declared that they were Alfred's, and took them up to London to put them on public display. Afterwards, they were brought back to Winchester, where they now lie under a plain stone slab just outside the east end of St Bartholomew's church.

Is this King Alfred's final resting place? Who knows.

This gravestone, lying just outside the east end of St Bartholomew's church, near the site of Hyde Abbey, may be the final resting place of King Alfred. It is marked by just a simple cross.

KING ALFRED AND THE BURNT CAKES

Very properly, Alfred the Great has become the icon of Winchester, so it is appropriate to conclude this book with an account of who he was and why he is called 'the Great'. Unfortunately many people only remember the story of how he burnt some cakes – a silly tale which is probably pure invention. So here, briefly, are some facts to remember when looking at the impressive statue which dominates the city today.

Three of Alfred's brothers had been Saxon kings before him. Then, after helping his brother King Ethelred to fight eight battles against the Danes, Alfred had the sadness of seeing him die of wounds after the Battle of Merton. Alfred was then elected king in place of Ethelred's sons.

The first few years of his reign were desperate. The Danes were moving further and further into the west of England. In January 878, they made a surprise attack and Alfred had to go into hiding in marshy land near Athelney, in Somerset. This is where the episode of 'Alfred and the burnt cakes' is supposed to have taken place. (Disguised as an ordinary traveller, he stayed for a while in a swineherd's cottage, and earned a sharp rebuke from the swineherd's wife after letting her cakes burn, which she had asked him to look after – not knowing, of course, who he was.)

Patiently, and with great courage and tenacity, Alfred gathered his army together again, and in May 878, he fought one of the most important battles in English history – the Battle of Edington, near Westbury in Wiltshire. There was ferocious fighting with swords and axes, lasting many hours. However, the Danes were decisively defeated, and the threat to Wessex was halted.

The most interesting thing about this victory was the way in which Alfred dealt with the defeated Danish leader Guthrum and the remains of his army. He could have slaughtered every one of them as they begged desperately for mercy. But astonishingly, Alfred insisted that Guthrum became baptised as a Christian, and stood as godfather to him; he then entertained the whole Danish army for twelve days and gave them gifts. After this he let them go, and enjoyed peace for fourteen years.

In 886, Alfred captured London, and in the subsequent peace treaty, he allowed the Danes to stay in East Anglia, but he kept Wessex and the south for himself.

In the following years of relative peace, Alfred showed himself to be an imaginative and innovative ruler; in fact, it has been said that if he had never fought a battle, he would still have been one of Britain's greatest kings.

During these final, fruitful years of his reign, Alfred reorganised the defences of Wessex and set up a rota system for military service, so that he could always have a standing army and yet men could also get on with their farming or other jobs in peace. He restored fortresses throughout Wessex and caused new ones to be built, thus founding dozens of new towns. These were 'boroughs' (the Saxon word burg means 'fort'). The largest of these in Wessex was his capital, Winchester.

Realising that the Danes would still attempt further invasions, he built large speedy ships, and successfully fought several sea battles. He is generally regarded as being the 'father of the English navy'.

In addition to all this, Alfred revised the laws of the land; introduced many new ones; invited foreign scholars to his court in Winchester; encouraged learning and the arts; set in motion the writing of the great Anglo-Saxon Chronicle; learnt Latin himself and translated books by Boethius, Bede, Gregory the Great, Orosius and St Augustine; invented a clock made with candles; and started the 'Book of Winchester' which was a survey of the countries, parishes and 'hundreds' into which he divided his kingdom.

Arguably, no other English king has had such a remarkable, energetic and wholly beneficial reign as that of Alfred – and yet he was only fifty when he died in Winchester in 899.

A thousand years later, his great reign was celebrated by the erection of the magnificent statue we see today in his capital city. His presence is felt here still.

Statue of King Alfred.

A WINCHESTER
TIME CHART

People have dwelt in the Winchester area for almost 2,500 years – or about 600 generations. In prehistoric times an Iron Age Celtic population had two settlements here: one at 'Oram's Arbour', slightly to the north of Westgate; and another on St Catherine's Hill, south of the city.

A succession of foreigners invaded and occupied the area. First a tribe from the continent known as the 'Belgae' – remembered in the name of present-day Belgium; then the Romans; then the Saxons; and finally the Normans, led by William the Conqueror.

The layout of present-day Winchester is almost exactly as the Romans had planned it. Its High Street is one of the oldest continuously used city streets in the country, following the earlier track used by Iron Age Celts.

PART ONE: WINCHESTER BEFORE 1066

BC

c. 400	Early Iron Age settlements on St Catherine's Hill and Oram's Arbour.
c. 50	Invasion by the Belgae, who were refugees from Gaul, escaping from the Romans.

AD

c. 43	The Romans capture Winchester from the Belgae, and call it 'Venta Belgarum' – 'Market-place of the Belgae.' It is the meeting point of five Roman roads.
c. 410	The Romans abandon Winchester and all troops and civilians return to Rome.
495	Cerdic, a pagan Saxon chieftain, invades Hampshire from the continent. With his son Cynric he wreaks havoc, killing Natanleod, a British king, in battle.
519	Cerdic, again with Cynric, wins another battle at Charford in Hampshire, and founds the kingdom of Wessex, choosing Winchester as his capital.
635	Birinus, an Italian Christian missionary, arrives in Britain. He converts King Cynegils (611–643), sixth king of Wessex, and becomes the first Bishop of the West Saxons, settling in Dorchester on Thames.

648   On Christmas Day, Birinus dedicates Winchester's first Christian church.
705   Bishop Daniel, sixth Bishop of the West Saxons, makes Winchester the
           centre of his diocese. From this date, therefore, Winchester becomes
           both the religious and secular capital of Wessex.
802   Egbert is crowned nineteenth King of Wessex in Winchester.
825   Egbert is acknowledged as 'Bretwalda', or 'King of Britain' by
           the other Saxon kingdoms – thus becoming first overall king of the
           English. From this date, Winchester can be regarded as the
           capital of England.
839   Egbert is buried in Old Minster. His remains are now in the present
           cathedral.
852   Swithun becomes Bishop of Winchester. He builds the city bridge and
           strong defensive walls around the city.
860   The Danes attack Winchester and burn down many buildings.
871–99   Reign of King Alfred, who makes Winchester a centre of learning and
           culture. He builds another monastery, called New Minster, next to the
           cathedral, which is now referred to as Old Minster.
c. 901   Alfred's widowed queen, Ealhswith, builds a nunnery called
           'Nunnaminster'. It is on the site of present day Abbey Gardens.
963–84   Aethelwold is Bishop of Winchester. His influence is profound. He
           rebuilds Old Minster, introduces Benedictine monks instead of married
           secular priests and makes St Swithun a cult figure, thus bringing
           thousands of pilgrims to the city.
1016–35   The Danish King Canute (Cnut) reigns in Winchester. As a devout
           Christian, he presents his crown and a large golden cross to Old
           Minster.
1042–66   The Saxon King Edward the Confessor reigns in Winchester. He is
           crowned in Old Minster on Easter Day, 3 April 1042 – the last English
           king to be crowned in any place other than Westminster Abbey.

Edward the Confessor spends much of his reign building Westminster Abbey,
and this results in a gradual shift of power and government from Winchester to
Westminster. Edward dies in January 1066 – just ten months before the Norman
Conquest and the destruction of Saxon England.

THE LEGEND OF COLBRAND, THE DANISH GIANT

According to Thomas Rudborne, a fifteenth-century monk of St Swithun's
Abbey, the city of Winchester was the prize fought for by two champions
fighting in single mortal combat in the reign of King Athelstan (924–39).
    The king of the Danes nominated a horrendous monster of a man named
Colbrand to be his champion – 'a giant wondrous of stature, hideous of aspect,

and of unparalleled ferocity'. For the Saxons, King Athelstan chose Guy of Warwick – 'self-restrained, resolute, manly in mind and skilled in combat'.

The battle was fought 'in a certain meadow lying northward of the city . . . called Denemarck' while Athelstan and his men watched from what is now North Walls. After many hours, Guy managed to cut off the head of giant Colbrand.

Today there is still an area called Danemark Mead. For many centuries the cathedral treasure contained 'The Axe of Colbrand', and well into the twentieth century there was a pub in Winchester called 'The Champions'.

PART TWO: WINCHESTER AFTER 1066

1066	William the Conqueror settles into Winchester, tearing down about sixty houses at the top of the main street to make way for his castle.
1079–93	Bishop William Walkelin builds a new Norman cathedral and Saxon Old Minster is completely demolished.
1100	William II ('Rufus') is killed in the New Forest and is buried in the cathedral. The population of Winchester is currently about 5,000.
1110	New Minster, built by Alfred the Great next to Old Minster, is demolished and the monks move to a new monastery – Hyde Abbey.
1136	Henry de Blois, Bishop of Winchester, founds the Hospital of St Cross – now the oldest almshouse in England.
1140	Civil war between King Stephen and his cousin, the Empress Matilda. What remains of Saxon Winchester is totally destroyed by fire.
1160	The 'Winchester Bible' is begun. This beautiful illuminated manuscript can be seen in the cathedral library – its greatest treasure.
1207	The future Henry III, son of King John, is born in Winchester.
1213	King John, having been excommunicated, is pardoned and renews his coronation oath in the old Chapter House.
1222	The castle's Great Hall is begun by Henry III – 'Henry of Winchester'.
c. 1250–80	'King Arthur's Table' is commissioned to be constructed.
1276	Edward I holds the first parliament in the Great Hall. More than twenty parliaments are held here by successive kings, until 1449.
1348	The Black Death ravages Winchester, returning in 1361, 1369, 1379 and finally in 1665–6. Before 1348, Winchester's population was about 8,000, but afterwards it was about 2,700.
1379	William of Wykeham founds New College, Oxford.
1382	William of Wykeham founds Winchester College.
1403	Henry IV marries his second wife, Joan of Navarre, in the cathedral.
1415	Henry V is entertained at Wolvesey on his way to victory at Agincourt.
1446	Cardinal Beaufort refounds the Hospital of St Cross, adding the new 'Order of Noble Poverty'. His 'Brothers' wear claret coloured gowns.

1486	Prince Arthur, son of Henry VII, is born in Winchester Castle and is baptised in the cathedral. Heir to the throne, he dies aged 15.
1522	Charles V, Holy Roman Emperor, visits Winchester. Henry VIII entertains him and shows him the Round Table, repainted for the occasion.
1538	St Swithun's shrine and all the monastery buildings are destroyed on the orders of Henry VIII. Hyde Abbey, Nunnaminster, and all other religious houses are also closed down and demolished.
1554	Queen Mary Tudor and Philip of Spain are married in the cathedral.
1603	Sir Walter Raleigh is tried for treason in the Great Hall and is condemned to death.
1642	Winchester is captured by the Parliamentarians in the Civil War, and Roundheads smash the cathedral windows and break up statues. The following year, 1643, Royalists recapture the city.
1645	Oliver Cromwell directs cannon fire on the city and recaptures it.
1651	Cromwellian soldiers demolish the castle, except for the Great Hall.
1665–6	Charles II brings his court to Winchester to escape the London plague. He asks Christopher Wren to design an impressive royal palace on the site of the former medieval castle.

THE STORY OF THOMAS KEN AND NELL GWYNN

The famous hymn writer, Thomas Ken (1631–1711), was a Fellow of Winchester College and a Prebend of Winchester Cathedral. 'Awake, my soul' and 'Glory to Thee, my God, this night' are two of his well-known hymns, written for the scholars of the College.

He lived in a house near the Deanery, now demolished (*see* plan on pp. 48–9), and when Charles II came to Winchester on one of his many visits, he requested that Ken give Nell Gwynn accommodation in his house. To everyone's horror, Ken refused point blank. He disapproved of mistresses and the King's immoral lifestyle. Charles was angry, but did not pursue his request.

However, a year or so later, when the next bishopric became vacant – that of Bath and Wells – Charles's respect for Ken's firm principles prompted him to give the bishopric to him, or, as Charles put it: '. . . to the ugly little man who wouldn't give poor Nelly a lodging.'

1685	Dame Alice Lisle is beheaded outside the present Eclipse Inn for sheltering two people trying to evade capture after the Monmouth Rebellion.
1713	A large clock is placed in High Street, together with a statue of Queen Anne, to celebrate the signing of the Treaty of Utrecht.
1754	The Obelisk near the Westgate is erected, commemorating the plagues.

1801	The first census is held. It records Winchester's population as being 6,194.
1817	Jane Austen, aged 41, dies on 18 July at No. 8 College Street.
1819	John Keats, aged 25, visits Winchester and writes his ode, 'To Autumn'.
1840	A railway line links Winchester to London and Southampton.
1841	The census for this year records Winchester's population as being 10,733.
1862	A Diocesan Training College for teachers is founded, later to become King Alfred's College.
1873	The newly constructed Guildhall is opened.
1894	Wren's palace, built for Charles II and subsequently used as military barracks, is destroyed by fire.
1901	The statue of Alfred the Great by Hamo Thorneycroft is erected in the Broadway, commemorating the 1,000th anniversary of his death – though in fact Alfred died in 899! The census for this year shows that Winchester's population has doubled since the census of 1841. The population now stands at 20,919.
1906–12	William Walker ('Diver Bill') and his team work to underpin the cathedral. Other necessary strengthening is undertaken, including the exterior buttresses against the south wall of the nave.
1923	A statue of Joan of Arc is placed in the cathedral.
1959	Cars and buses enter and depart from Winchester through the narrow arch of the Westgate for the last time.
1960	New County Council Offices are opened near Westgate.
1962	A new shrine in memory of St Swithun is set up in the cathedral to commemorate the 1,000th anniversary of his death.
1971	Winchester's population is now 31,107.
1974	The Law Courts are moved from the medieval Great Hall to a new flint-and-stone building adjoining it.
1975	Elisabeth Frink's statue, 'Horse and Rider', is erected in High Street.
1979	Queen Elizabeth II distributes the Royal Maundy in Winchester Cathedral to commemorate the 900th anniversary of its foundation.
1985	Queen Elizabeth the Queen Mother opens 'Queen Eleanor's Garden' adjoining the Great Hall.
1990	The Brooks Shopping Centre is completed.
2001	The population of Winchester now stands at 37,500.
2004	The restoration of the City Mill is completed by the National Trust, and flour is produced there for the first time in over ninety years.
2005	King Alfred's College, which was renamed University College in 2004, is now renamed again and becomes the University of Winchester. It is the newest university in Britain, and its lecture theatre, 'The Stripe', is formally opened in November. There are 3,000 full-time and 2,500 part-time students.

As you leave Winchester towards Romsey, look back at the Westgate and enjoy the pair of gargoyle-like carved heads – one on each side, above the former portcullis. Out of their wide-open mouths came the chains which used to raise and lower the drawbridge. The head shown in this picture is on the left side of the gate.

SELECTED BOOKLIST

Many books and pamphlets on Winchester are on sale in the cathedral shop and in the Tourist Information Office in the Guildhall. Also, it's worth searching in second-hand bookshops for the many books on Winchester which are now, unfortunately, out of print. Here is a selection of books consulted in compiling *Winchester Curiosities*:

Biddle, Martin, *King Arthur's Round Table*, The Boydell Press, Woodbridge, 2000

Birt, Raymond, *The Glories of Winchester Cathedral*, Winchester Publications Ltd, London, 1948

Bussby, Frederick, *Winchester Cathedral 1079–1979*, Paul Cave Publications Ltd, Southampton, 1979

Carpenter Turner, Barbara, *A History of Winchester*, Phillimore & Co. Ltd, Chichester, 1992

Leach, Arthur F., *A History of Winchester College*, Duckworth & Co., London, 1899

Peddie, John, *Alfred, Warrior King*, Sutton Publishing Ltd, Stroud, 1999

Sabben-Clare, James, *Winchester College*, Paul Cave Publications Ltd, Southampton, 1981

Varley, The Revd Telford, *Winchester*, Adam and Charles Black, London, 1910

Vesey-Fitzgerald, Brian, *Winchester*, Phoenix House Ltd, London, 1953

Williamson, Hugh Ross, *The Ancient Capital: An Historian in Search of Winchester*, Frederick Muller Ltd, London, 1953

SELECTED WEBSITES

Cathedral	www.winchester-cathedral.org.uk
	www.clara.net/reedhome/winchester
City of Winchester	www.cityofwinchester.co.uk
	www.winchester.co.uk
	www.visitwinchester.co.uk
	www.nationaltrust.org.uk/places/winchester
	www.winchestermilitarymuseums.co.uk
	www.hants.gov.uk/greathall
Winchester College	www.winchestercollege.org.uk

INDEX

ABOUT THE AUTHOR

DAVID HILLIAM has written several other books for The History Press: *Kings, Queens, Bones & Bastards*; *Monarchs, Murderers & Mistresses*; *Crown, Orb & Sceptre*; and, most recently, *A Salisbury Miscellany*. He grew up in Salisbury, but moved to Winchester in the early 1950s, when traffic still passed through the Westgate. After Cambridge and Oxford, he taught in Versailles, Canterbury and Bournemouth. He is now a freelance writer and lecturer living in Dorset. He still has an Edward III penny which he dug up in his parents' garden in Winchester's parish of Weeke – it brings back happy memories of many hours exploring the hidden nooks and crannies of Winchester, ancient capital of Wessex.